Read and Respond Journal

GRADE 3

Copyright © by Houghton Mifflin Harcourt Publishing Company

All rights reserved. No part of this work may be reproduced or transmitted in any form or by any means, electronic or mechanical, including photocopying or recording, or by any information storage or retrieval system, without the prior written permission of the copyright owner unless such copying is expressly permitted by federal copyright law.

Permission is hereby granted to individuals using the corresponding student's textbook or kit as the major vehicle for regular classroom instruction to photocopy entire pages from this publication in classroom quantities for instructional use and not for resale. Requests for information on other matters regarding duplication of this work should be submitted through our Permissions website at https://customercare.hmhco.com/contactus/Permissions.html or mailed to Houghton Mifflin Harcourt Publishing Company, Attn: Intellectual Property Licensing, 9400 Southpark Center Loop, Orlando, Florida 32819-8647.

Printed in the U.S.A.

ISBN 978-0-358-25227-6

11 2023

4500879844 r6.23

If you have received these materials as examination copies free of charge, Houghton Mifflin Harcourt Publishing Company retains title to the materials and they may not be resold. Resale of examination copies is strictly prohibited.

Possession of this publication in print format does not entitle users to convert this publication, or any portion of it, into electronic format.

Contents

MODULE 1
- Not Just a Little! 2
- Icos Goes to School 10
- Swedish Meatball Potstickers with Mustard Dipping Sauce 18

MODULE 2
- Building a New Barn 26
- Douglas Florian's Books 34
- Living Things are Linked 42

MODULE 3
- Snow Petrels 50
- The Life of a Hickory Tree 58
- Puppets Around the World 66

MODULE 4
- To the South Seas 74
- Mark's Idea 82
- The Rockets 90

MODULE 5
- Little Mud-Face 98
- Dog of the Future 106
- The Race of 1903 114

MODULE 6
- A World of Ice 122
- Mammoths Long Ago and Today 130
- Dogs That Help 138

MODULE 7
- Climbing the Slopes 146
- The Trial of John Peter Zenger 154
- Sprinting Joyce 162

MODULE 8
- The Boy Who Made the TV 170
- Anansi's Bad Hair Day 178
- Ski Patrol 186

MODULE 9
- Let's Play Ball 194
- Aleck's Big Ideas 202
- Owls 210

MODULE 10
- Sports, Exactly 218
- The Jimjick King 226
- The Enchanted Flute 234

MODULE 1 WEEK 1

Not Just a Little!

by Lois Grippo

Bob loved to make good things to eat. He grew wheat and vegetables on his farm. He had chickens. He used them to make yummy meals. Still, it was no fun cooking for just himself. It was no fun eating alone.

Bob wanted to share his food with his neighbors. He wanted to sit around a big table. He wanted to laugh and have fun.

READ & RESPOND

Theme

Why does Bob want to eat with his neighbors?

_____
_____
_____

Bob called his neighbor Luis. "Can you come to my house for dinner?" Bob asked.

"I cannot leave the store," Luis said. "I am staying open late to earn more money."

Luis sold fruit and vegetables. He never made time to talk or have fun. Bob called his other neighbors. They were busy, too. Bob sat on his porch and thought. He tried to figure out a way to get his neighbors together.

READ & RESPOND

Make and Confirm Predictions

Do you think Bob will get his neighbors together? Explain.

_____
_____
_____

Bob came up with a plan. He cooked chicken in a pot. It smelled very good. Bob went to the park with his pot of chicken.

Bob walked past Luis's store. The door was open. Luis smelled the chicken. He came outside and saw Bob.

"What is making that good smell?" Luis asked.

"The smell is the chicken in my pot," said Bob.

READ & RESPOND

Make and Confirm Predictions

Why do you think Bob takes his chicken to the park?

_____

_____

_____

"There is a picnic at four o'clock," Bob said. "You must come! You can bring some food. Tell your customers to come, too."

"I am too busy for a picnic. I have to work," said Luis. Then he smelled the chicken again. "Maybe I will close the store early. I can bring a little corn to the picnic."

"No, no! Not just a little!" said Bob. "Bring lots of corn!"

READ & RESPOND

Theme

What makes Luis change his mind about going to the picnic?

_____
_____
_____

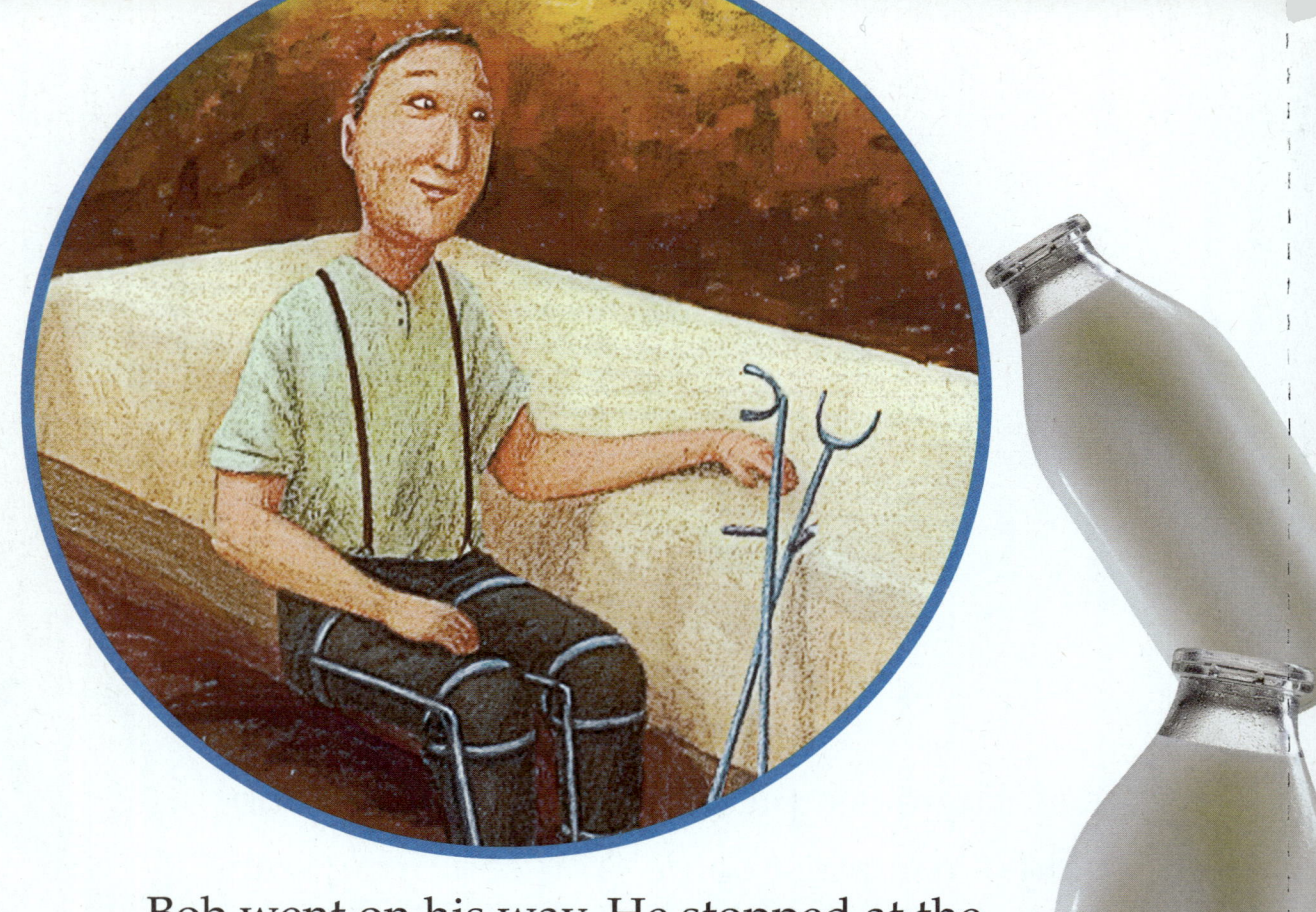

Bob went on his way. He stopped at the library. He stopped at the hardware store. Everyone smelled Bob's chicken. They all wanted to come to the picnic.

At last, Bob arrived at the park. He put his chicken on the table. Bob's neighbor Lee came by.

READ & RESPOND

Make and Confirm Predictions

Do you think everyone will come to the picnic? Why, or why not?

_____

_____

_____

"Luis contacted me. He told me there is a picnic. I will bring a little bit of milk," Lee said.

"No, no! Not just a little!" said Bob. "Bring lots of milk."

At four o'clock, Lee came back to the park. He brought lots of milk. Luis came to the park with lots of corn.

READ & RESPOND Make and Confirm Predictions

Why do you think Bob is telling people to bring more than just a little?

_____
_____
_____

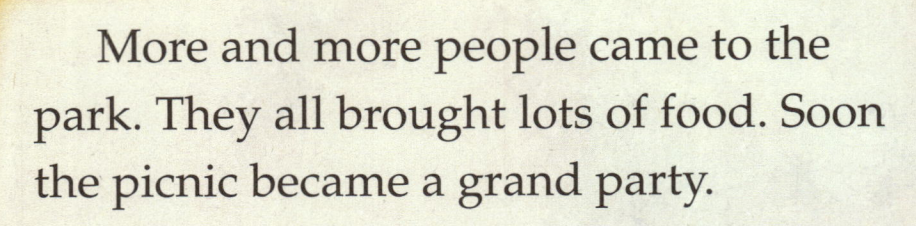

More and more people came to the park. They all brought lots of food. Soon the picnic became a grand party.

Everyone had fun. Everyone talked and laughed together. Bob was happy. His plan worked just fine.

READ & RESPOND

Theme

How do Bob's neighbors change by the end of the story?

Reread and Respond

1 **Write three things to tell about Bob.**

_____

_____

_____

> **Hint**
> Look for clues on page 2.

2 **How did Bob get his neighbors together?**

_____

_____

_____

> **Hint**
> Reread the story to help you.

3 **What is the theme of the story?**

_____

_____

_____

> **Hint**
> Think about what the characters learned.

MODULE 1 WEEK 2

Icos Goes to School
by Margaret Maugenest

Morning, 400 B.C.E.
Athens, Greece

Doran shook the sleeping boy. "Time to get up, Icos," he said. "It's going to be fine, sunny weather."

Icos yawned and turned over. "It's always fine weather in Athens," he said. "So what?"

"You must get up," Doran said firmly. "It's time for school."

READ & RESPOND

Literary Elements

When and where does the story take place?

_____

_____

_____

Icos sighed. It was barely light out. He didn't want to get up. It took him a while to get out of bed.

Doran walked to school with Icos. Doran was Icos's servant. The two strolled through the streets.

They reached the school late. The teacher was already sitting on his tall chair. Icos sat on a bench at the back. Doran stayed outside.

READ & RESPOND

Literary Elements

What problem does Icos have?

_____
_____
_____

The teacher gave each student a block of wax. It was time to practice writing. Icos looked for his stylus.

Doran came in with the stylus. Now Icos could carve letters into the wax. Icos tried not to yawn. He was proud of his tidy writing. He wanted to do a good job.

READ & RESPOND

Literary Elements

Describe Icos. What does he look like? How does he act?

_____

_____

_____

By now, Icos was wide awake. It was time to learn a poem. This poem was not written down. The teacher spoke each line. The students repeated it.

The teacher called on Icos to say the whole poem. Icos stood. He spoke in a firm voice. He did not leave one word out.

Doran came in. He took the writing stylus back. "You certainly did well!" he told Icos.

READ & RESPOND

Literary Elements

Is Doran a good friend to Icos? Explain.

_____

_____

_____

Now it was music time. One student played the harp. Another played the flute. Icos and the other boys sang.

Icos looked out at the servants. Doran was nodding in time to the music. The teacher was tapping his foot. "We must be doing well," Icos thought.

READ & RESPOND

Literary Elements

What does Icos think of school now? How do you know?

_____

_____

_____

The afternoon was for sports. The boys walked to the sports field. Their servants came with them. The field was at the edge of the city.

The boys worked hard. Building strong bodies was important. They ran races. They jumped. Sports teachers watched them. Icos won a race. He was very pleased.

READ & RESPOND

Literary Elements

Where do the boys practice sports? What time do they practice?

_____

_____

_____

At last the school day ended. Icos and Doran walked home together. "That was a full day," Icos said.

"Yes, it was," Doran agreed. "You had fun at school, didn't you?" he asked.

Icos knew what Doran was saying. "Yes, I did. I'll try not to be so slow and grumpy tomorrow morning!"

READ & RESPOND

Literary Elements

Does Icos still have a problem? Explain.

_____
_____
_____

Reread and Respond

1 **Name one way that Doran is helpful to Icos.**

_____

_____

_____

> **Hint**
> For clues, see pages 10, 12, and 13.

2 **How does Icos change at the end of the story?**

_____

_____

_____

> **Hint**
> For clues, see page 16.

3 **What clues in the pictures show that the story takes place long ago?**

_____

_____

_____

> **Hint**
> Clues are on every page.

MODULE 1
WEEK 3

Swedish Meatball Potstickers with Mustard Dipping Sauce

by Margaret Maugenest

Ava's class was having a food fair. Ava was on the planning team. She came home after the meeting. She threw her bag down. She slumped in a chair. She looked glum.

READ & RESPOND

Point of View

Look at the pronouns on this page. What do they tell you about the narrator's point of view?

_____

_____

"What's the matter?" her mom asked.

"I have to bring food for the fair," said Ava. "The food must tell about my family. I can only bring one dish."

"Make your Chinese potstickers. They're yummy!" Mom remarked.

"I don't want to. I make them all the time," said Ava.

Potstickers

READ & RESPOND

Make Inferences

How does Ava feel? How do you know?

_____
_____
_____

"What about Grandma Ida's Swedish meatballs? She made them in Sweden," said Mom. "She still makes them."

Ava shook her head. "I like the meatballs," she said. "I just don't want to make them for the food fair."

No dish sounded right. Ava looked at her mom anxiously. What could Ava bring?

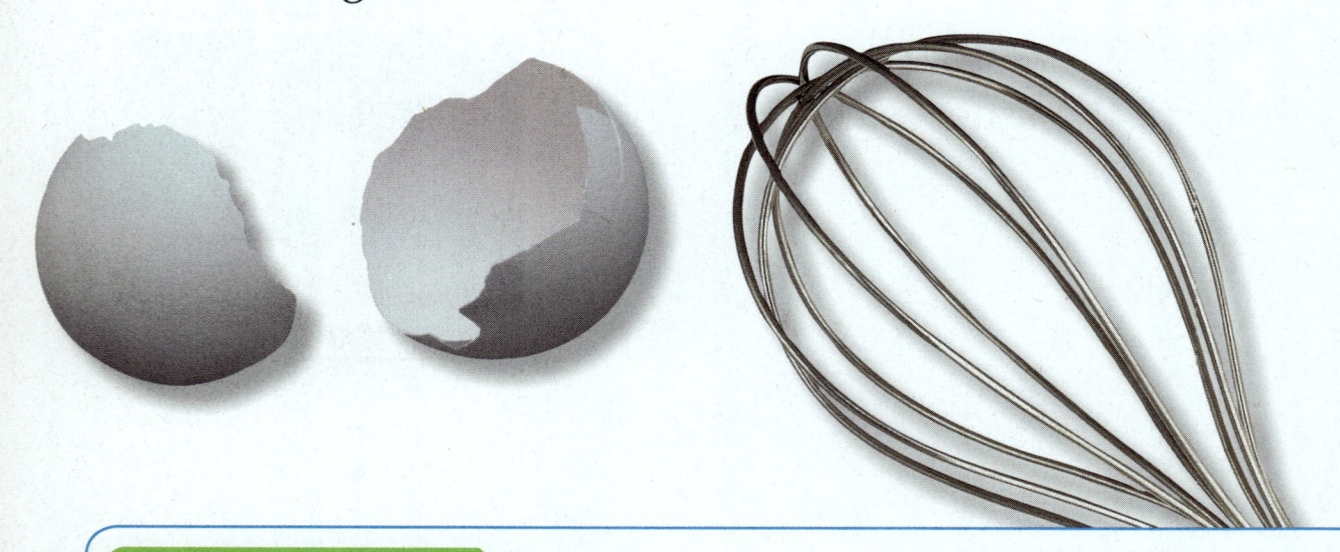

READ & RESPOND

Point of View

What clues on this page help you to know the point of view of the narrator?

_____

_____

"What about Dad's side of the family?" Mom said. "They came from Poland. You can make Polish food. Dad's mom was a great cook. I have her recipes."

Ava's mom got a folder. "Let's see. There is Polish stuffed cabbage. There is fish spread. There is mustard dipping sauce, too. These foods are easy to make. They are also very tasty!"

READ & RESPOND

Make Inferences

How can you tell that Ava's mom wants to be helpful?

_____
_____
_____

Ava was not listening. She stared at the floor. Her face had a big frown. She was tense and worried.

"What's the matter?" Mom asked.

"I can only bring one dish. I don't have a one-dish story! There is more than one part of me. There's the part that was born in China. Then there's the Swedish part, from you. There's also the Polish part from Dad!"

READ & RESPOND

Make Inferences

What does Ava mean when she says she doesn't have a one-dish story?

_____
_____
_____

Mom gave Ava a big hug. "Don't worry. We will find the perfect dish to tell your story," she said.

"A combo dish?" asked Ava.

"Yes. Let's think of something new," said Mom.

Ava's eyes lit up. There was a big smile on her face.

READ & RESPOND

Make Inferences

How does Ava feel now? How do you know?

_____

_____

_____

"How about Polish stuffed cabbage? I can make it with Chinese soy sauce and Swedish jam," Ava said.

"I'm not sure about the jam," said Mom. "Could we do potstickers with fish spread?"

"Yech!" said Ava. Then she smiled. "I know! I'll make Swedish meatball potstickers with mustard dipping sauce."

"That sounds great!" said Mom. "Let's get the ingredients and start!"

READ & RESPOND

Point of View

Is this story told in first-person or third-person point of view? How do you know?

Reread and Respond

1 **Write two words that tell about Ava's mom.**

_____

_____

_____

> **Hint**
> Clues you can use are on almost every page!

2 **What are the different parts of Ava's family background?**

_____

_____

_____

> **Hint**
> For a clue, see page 22.

3 **Why is Ava happy to make a combo dish?**

_____

_____

_____

> **Hint**
> For a clue, see page 23.

Building a New Barn

by Margaret Maugenest

The farmer looks at her barn. Once, the barn looked good. The wood boards were straight. The roof was strong.

Now the barn is old. The planks sag. The roof is sinking in. The paint is chipped.

The farmer is not happy. She wants to build a new barn.

READ & RESPOND

Main Ideas and Details

Why does the farmer want to build a new barn?

_____
_____
_____

Getting Started

A crew of helpers comes. Some of the workers are from town. Some of them come from other farms. They are all ready to work!

First, they tear down the old barn. The workers take away the used planks.

Some people chop down nearby trees. They saw the wood into planks. The new planks will be used to build the barn.

READ & RESPOND

Retell

What is the first thing the workers do?

_____
_____
_____

Everyone Helps!

Some people will build the barn. There are other jobs, too. The workers will get hungry. So some people will make lunch for them.

A few workers brought their children. The children watch. They will see how a barn is built. Some day they may build a barn.

READ & RESPOND Main Ideas and Details

Why doesn't everyone help build the barn?

_____

_____

_____

The Work Begins

To begin, workers place big blocks of stone in the ground. These will make the base of the barn.

Next, the builders make a frame for each wall. They measure the wood. Then they saw it into pieces.

The pieces are joined together. The team uses nails. The nails are metal. Sometimes they use pegs. The pegs are carved from wood.

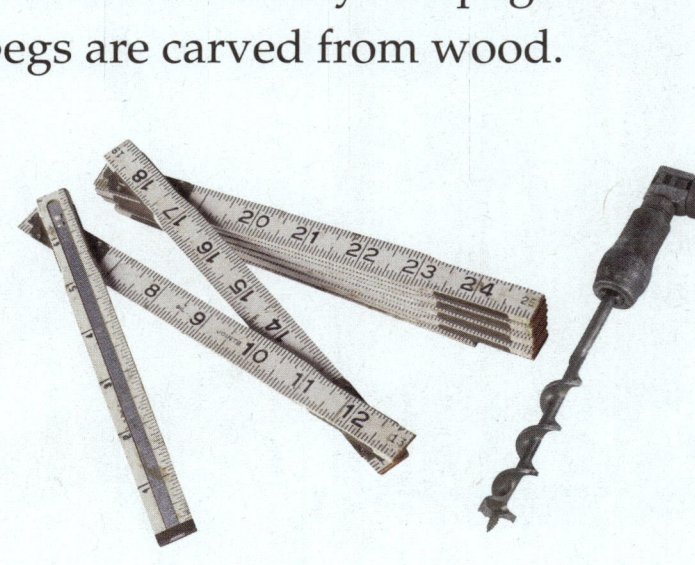

READ & RESPOND

Retell

Explain how the builders make the frames for the barn.

_____

_____

_____

Step by Step

Soon it is time to raise the barn. Workers lift the frames by hand. It is hard work. They need help. So other workers use long poles to push the frames into place.

The top comes next. Some workers climb the frame. They must be good at balancing on the frame so they do not fall off.

READ & RESPOND

Main Ideas and Details

How are the frames raised and pushed into place?

_____
_____
_____

The workers pull up long planks of wood. The planks stretch across the top of the barn. They fit into slots in the frame.

All the parts are nailed down. Now the roof will be very strong. Some barn roofs are slanted. Others are curved. This roof is curved.

READ & RESPOND

Retell

What happens after the workers fit the wood planks into the frame?

_____
_____
_____

A New Barn!

The workers stop for lunch. Then they go back to work. It is almost dark when the last nail is hammered into place. The workers feel excitement. They are happy and smiling. The barn is finished!

The new barn looks great. The farmer is very happy. She thanks everyone.

The workers are tired. They walk to their cars and trucks, and they go home.

READ & RESPOND

Retell

Explain how to build a barn. Use the story to help you.

_____

_____

_____

Reread and Respond

1 **Compare what the children do with what the grownups do.**

_____

_____

_____

> **Hint**
> For clues, see page 28.

2 **How does the farmer feel at the beginning of the story? How does she feel at the end? Why?**

_____

_____

_____

> **Hint**
> For clues, see pages 26 and 32.

3 **How do you think the workers on the team began learning how to build barns?**

_____

_____

_____

> **Hint**
> For clues, see page 28.

MODULE 2 WEEK 2

Douglas Florian's Books

by Gail Mack

The Boy Who Loved Drawing

Douglas Florian wasn't the first artist in his family. His dad was.

Douglas's dad loved to make sketches of things in nature. He showed Douglas how to draw. He taught Douglas how to look closely at nature.

READ & RESPOND Main Ideas and Details

Who taught Douglas how to draw?
_____
_____
_____

Drawing was fun for Douglas. When he was ten years old, he entered a coloring contest. His art won second place. His prize was a pair of roller skates.

READ & RESPOND

Text and Graphic Features

How does the picture help you to know what roller skates are?

_____
_____
_____

35

An Art Student

One summer, Douglas took an art class. He loved it. He learned to use different art tools. Artists use many tools. They might use paint or pen and ink. They might even use chalk.

Douglas was just fifteen years old. He already knew what he wanted to become. He was going to be an artist.

READ & RESPOND

Main Ideas and Details

What kinds of tools might an artist use?

_____
_____
_____

A Working Artist

Douglas did become an artist. He sold his drawings to magazines and newspapers. He made art for children's books, too.

At first, he would illustrate other people's stories. Later, he wrote his own stories. His first books were about nature. Douglas filled them with drawings of things like frogs, turtles, and shells.

READ & RESPOND

Main Ideas and Details

What did Douglas do as an artist?

_____

_____

_____

A Writer of Poems

One day, Douglas saw a book of silly poems. He smiled as he turned the pages. "A book like this would be fun to make!" he thought.

So he wrote some poems. He used funny sounds and silly words. He made enough poems to fill a book. Then he drew pictures for the poems.

COO-COO

READ & RESPOND

Text and Graphic Features

How does the picture show a funny sound?

_____
_____
_____

A Winner

Douglas liked to imagine made-up animals. He wrote a book of poems about them. After that, he wrote a book of poems about real animals. It was called *Beast Feast*. His books were a big hit. One book even won an award!

Douglas still loves making art and writing poems. His books make kids laugh.

READ & RESPOND Text and Graphic Features

What detail in the text does the picture of Douglas Florian show?

_____

_____

_____

Douglas Florian Timeline

This timeline shows events in Douglas Florian's life.

1950	Douglas Florian is born.
1960	He wins second prize in an art contest.
1965	He decides to become an artist.
Around 1970	He studies art in college.
1994	His poem book, *Beast Feast*, comes out.
1995	*Beast Feast* wins the Lee Bennett Hopkins Poetry Award.

READ & RESPOND

Text and Graphic Features

What is one event on the timeline that you don't read about anywhere else in this story?

_____
_____

Reread and Respond

1 **What did Douglas Florian do after he made pictures for other people's stories?**

_____

_____

_____

> **Hint**
> Look on page 37.

2 **How did Douglas Florian's dad help him become an artist?**

_____

_____

_____

> **Hint**
> Look on page 34.

3 **Write three words that tell about Douglas Florian's art. Explain.**

_____

_____

_____

> **Hint**
> Clues are on almost every page!

MODULE 2 WEEK 3

Living Things Are Linked

A RETELLING OF AN AFRICAN TALE

by Dina McClellan

Once there was a chief who was a stern ruler. He demanded that all in the village obey him. The people in the village always did as the chief wished.

Only one person was not afraid of the chief. That was his grandmother. She did not follow all the chief's rules and she spoke her mind.

READ & RESPOND

Literary Elements

Describe the chief. How do the other characters in the story feel about him?

_____

_____

42

One night the chief couldn't sleep. The frogs outside were making too much noise. This was a serious problem for the chief.

He woke up all the people in the village. "If I can't sleep, no one will sleep," he said. "Get rid of all the frogs!"

READ & RESPOND

Visualize

What words on this page help you to visualize the frogs?

_____
_____
_____

So the people caught all the frogs. They moved them to a different village. Later they felt sad. They did not think the frogs should have to move. The people were afraid of the chief.

Only the chief's grandmother was not afraid. "You'll be sorry," she said. "All living things are linked. Even you and the frogs."

The chief had to laugh. "How could frogs be linked to a big chief like me?" he said.

READ & RESPOND

Literary Elements

List two big events that happen on this page of the story.

_____
_____
_____

Soon it was time for the harvest. Everyone in the village had to gather beans and sweet potatoes. It was hard to work outdoors. The air was full of mosquitoes. Thousands of them!

The chief stayed in his hut while others worked. The mosquitoes found him there. He couldn't sleep or think. There was too much buzzing! The chief was covered with bites.

READ & RESPOND

Visualize

Reread this page. What would you hear, see, taste, smell, or feel if you lived in the village?

_____

_____

"Get rid of the mosquitoes!" the chief said. "I want every last one gone by morning!"

"Why didn't you take my advice?" said the grandmother. "We are in this mess because you made the people move the frogs."

The chief paid no attention to her. Again he told the villagers to get rid of the mosquitoes.

READ & RESPOND

Literary Elements

What problem does the chief have now? What is his solution?

_____

_____

_____

People did their best. Still, they couldn't move mosquitoes like they could move frogs. There were too many. The next day there were even more.

The chief gave another order. "This time, move them ALL!" he said.

The people tried again. They did their best. They still couldn't get rid of all the mosquitoes. There were just too many.

READ & RESPOND

Visualize

How do you think the chief feels when he sees that there are more mosquitoes than ever? Which words help you to know?

_____

_____

"You should have left those frogs alone," said the grandmother.

"What are you talking about?" said the chief. He was very upset.

"Don't you know that frogs eat mosquitoes? That's why you need frogs!" the grandmother said.

At last, the chief learned his lesson. He found out the hard way that all living things are linked.

READ & RESPOND

Literary Elements

How does the story end? Does the chief change? Explain.

_____
_____
_____

Reread and Respond

1 Is the chief a good listener? How can you tell?

_____

_____

_____

> **Hint**
> For clues, look on pages 42, 44, and 46.

2 Why do the people do whatever the chief tells them to do?

_____

_____

_____

> **Hint**
> For clues, look on pages 42 and 44.

3 How is the chief's grandmother unlike the other characters in the story?

_____

_____

_____

> **Hint**
> For clues, look on pages 42 and 44.

Snow Petrels

by Margaret Maugenest

Winter in Antarctica

Antarctica is a chilly place at the South Pole. It is the coldest place on Earth. Ice covers the ground all year.

Winter in Antarctica begins in June. The days are very short. There is no light in the sky. It is dark all of the time. Few animals live in Antarctica. There is little food. Survival is very hard.

READ & RESPOND

Central Idea

Look at the title of the text. What do you think this text will be about?

_____
_____
_____

Warming Up

Spring comes in September. The days get longer. The sun shines into the sea. The sea becomes rich with small plants.

More animals come. Little animals called krill swim by. They eat the plants. Bigger fish come. They eat the plants and the krill.

Other animals come. There is plenty of food. Seals, whales, and birds hunt smaller animals. They eat krill and fish.

Sea plants

Small fish

READ & RESPOND

Text Structure

How are the days in spring different from the days in winter?

_____

_____

_____

Summer Days

Summer begins in December. Whales migrate to the Antarctic waters. They feed on the krill.

Now the sea is full of life. Flying birds come. They make nests on the shore.

Some of these birds are petrels. Petrels are like sea gulls. Their strong wings let them fly far from land. Their thick coats keep them warm. Most birds can't smell. Petrels can. They sniff out a meal.

READ & RESPOND

Central Idea

Think about the title. What details on this page link back to the central idea?

_____

_____

Robin

Snow petrel

Snow Petrel Facts

Snow petrels are much smaller than other petrels. They are about the size of robins. Their feathers are white. They blend in with the snowy landscape. Only their bills, eyes, and feet are dark. When they fly, they flutter like bats.

READ & RESPOND

Central Idea

How does the heading on this page help you know the central idea?

_____
_____
_____

Habits of Snow Petrels

Snow petrels are shy. If bothered, they may just fly away. If something gets too close, they have a trick. They spit out a liquid that smells very bad!

These birds fly low over the sea to find food. When they see their dinner, they dive into the water to catch it. Some birds roll in dust to clean their feathers. Snow petrels roll in the snow. That is how they clean up after they hunt.

READ & RESPOND

Text Structure

Think about how some birds clean their feathers. What is different about how snow petrels do it?

_____

_____

Petrel Families

A snow petrel finds a partner. Then the pair makes a nest. Like all birds, snow petrels look for a spot safe from other animals. Petrels make their nests in holes on rocky cliffs.

Most birds make their nests with leaves and grass. It's hard to find leaves or grass in Antarctica. Snow petrels line their nests with small pebbles.

The female lays one egg. Six weeks later, the chick hatches. In seven more weeks, it will fly away. It may live up to twenty years.

READ & RESPOND

Text Structure

How is a snow petrel nest different from the nests of most birds?

_____
_____
_____

The North Pole (Arctic) and South Pole (Antarctic)

- In this diagram, the North Pole is at the top of Earth. The South Pole is at the bottom.

- The North Pole and the South Pole stay dark during the winter. They stay light during the summer.

- The North Pole and the South Pole are very cold places.

When Different Seasons Begin in the North and South Poles				
	Winter	**Spring**	**Summer**	**Fall**
North Pole	December	March	June	September
South Pole	June	September	December	March

READ & RESPOND

Text Structure and Central Idea

How does the author organize the text? How does it help you understand the central idea?

_____

_____

Reread and Respond

1 **How is life in Antarctica different in winter than in spring and summer?**

_____
_____
_____

> **Hint**
> For clues, see pages 50, 51, and 52.

2 **Birds, seals, and whales come to Antarctica in the summer. Why don't they live there in the winter?**

_____
_____
_____

> **Hint**
> For clues, see pages 50 and 56.

3 **How is the snow petrel different from other birds?**

_____
_____
_____

> **Hint**
> For clues, see pages 52, 53, 54, and 55.

MODULE 3 WEEK 2

The Life of a Hickory Tree

by Dina McClellan

It is fall in the forest. Squirrels are busy. They are looking for nuts. They need to store the nuts. They save them to eat in the winter.

This squirrel does not save all the nuts. He eats one now. He cracks the shell. Then he eats the tasty nut.

READ & RESPOND

Summarize

Why do squirrels need to save the nuts?

_____
_____
_____

A Lucky Nut

Another squirrel finds a hickory nut. He hears a noise. He drops the nut and runs away.

The nut hits a stone. It bounces to the ground. Soon, leaves fall on the nut. They hide it.

This is a lucky nut. It will grow into a hickory tree. Most other nuts will not. Squirrels and other animals will eat them.

READ & RESPOND

Summarize

Does the heading "A Lucky Nut" tell about the text on this page? How?

Hidden from Sight

Even bears like to eat hickory nuts. They eat them whenever they can.

Bears do not find this hidden nut. The shell of the nut rots. During winter, the nut sinks into the soil.

Animals are looking for food in the forest. Rabbits and mice do not find the nut. It is buried deep in the ground.

READ & RESPOND

Content-Area Words

Think about the words "winter," "animals," and "forest." What subject area do these words come from?

_____

_____

The Seed Sprouts

It is spring in the forest. The seed inside the nut sprouts. It grows roots. They go deep into the ground. The roots absorb water from the soil.

The little tree grows. Years pass. The big hickory tree makes more nuts. Most of them never sprout.

READ & RESPOND

Content-Area Words

Where else have you heard the words "roots," "sprouts," and "soil"? Does that help you understand what is happening in the text?

_____

_____

A Growing Tree

Time passes. After ten years, the tree is seven feet tall. It is as thick as a man's thumb.

The leaves grow in clumps of five. They are light green in the summer. In the fall, they turn yellow.

The tree faces many dangers. It can be chopped down. Fires can hurt it. Bugs may make holes in it. Birds may peck the holes and make them bigger.

READ & RESPOND Summarize

What does the heading tell you about the information on this page?

_____
_____
_____

Getting Older

More time passes. After twenty years, the bark is still smooth. Now the tree is thirty years old. Its coverings start to split. Each part of the bark is tight in the middle. The edges curve away from the trunk. This makes the tree look shaggy.

After forty years, the first nuts appear. Some of the nuts take root. They might grow into trees. Hickory trees can live for 300 years!

READ & RESPOND

Summarize

Write one sentence that summarizes the information on this page.

_____

_____

_____

The Cycle Goes On

It's fall in the forest. A squirrel comes out. It knows when the hickory tree has nuts. The squirrel looks for them.

Other animals look for nuts, too. Will they find all of the nuts? Will one lucky nut sprout in the spring?

Throughout the forest, trees are growing. Each one is in a different stage of life.

READ & RESPOND

Content-Area Words

Look at the heading on this page. Do you know about any other "cycles"? List one.

_____

_____

Reread and Respond

1 Which kinds of animals look for hickory nuts?

_____

_____

_____

> **Hint**
> For clues, see the sections called "A Lucky Nut" and "Hidden from Sight."

2 How does the hickory tree get water from the soil?

_____

_____

_____

> **Hint**
> For clues, see the section that has a heading about sprouting.

3 Look at the trees on the first and last pages of the story. Why do they look similar?

_____

_____

_____

> **Hint**
> Think about the story. Read the headings to remind yourself about the tree's life.

MODULE 3 WEEK 3

Puppets Around the World

by Lois Grippo

People love puppets! They are a familiar toy. Children all around the world love to play with them.

The first puppets may have been made in Egypt. These puppets were simple toys. They were made of wood. Strings made their parts move.

READ & RESPOND

Author's Purpose

Based on the title, do you think this text is going to persuade you, inform you, or entertain you? Explain.

_____
_____

Shadow Puppets

Long ago, people in Southeast Asia made shadow puppets. These puppets were flat. They were made from paper. Each puppet was attached to a stick. Moving the stick made the puppet move.

The puppets were held behind a silk screen. Candles were lit to make shadows.

People sat on the other side of the screen. They could not see the puppets. They could not see the people holding them. They saw large puppet shadows on the silk screen!

READ & RESPOND

Central Idea

Look at the heading on this page. How does it help you to know the central idea?

_____
_____

Bunraku Puppets

The Japanese also make special puppets. They are called Bunraku puppets. These puppets are large. They can be as big as a person.

It takes three people to move these puppets. The people appear on stage with the puppet.

The puppet's movements are never jerky. People work hard to make the puppets move smoothly.

> **READ & RESPOND**
>
> Central Idea
>
> **List two facts about Bunraku puppets.**
> _____
> _____
> _____

Hand Puppets

Did you ever make a sock puppet? A sock puppet is a hand puppet.

There were hand puppets long ago in China. These puppets were not made from socks. They were made from wood. The wood was hollow. A person's hand fit inside.

| READ & RESPOND | Author's Purpose |

Think about what you have read so far. Have you learned anything new? Explain.

_____

_____

Puppet Theaters

Puppet shows are done on small stages. Sometimes the stage is vacant. Often it is filled. There may be trees and homes. There may be hills and farms.

Puppets race across the stage. They peek out of windows. Fans give applause when a hero fights a dragon. They boo when the dragon fights back. Puppet shows are fun.

READ & RESPOND

Central Idea

How does the information on this page help you to understand the central idea?

_____

_____

Puppet Shows

What are puppet shows about? Some teach a lesson. Some tell the history of a place. Long ago there were no TVs. There were no newspapers. People learned the news from puppet shows.

So listen closely to puppets! They can be very funny. They can also tell you things you did not know!

READ & RESPOND

Central Idea

Write one sentence that tells the central idea of this text.

_____

_____

_____

Make a Sock Puppet

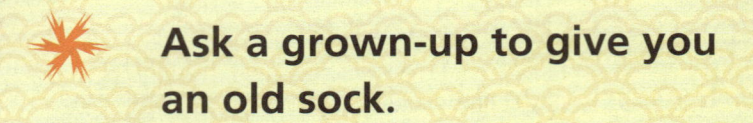

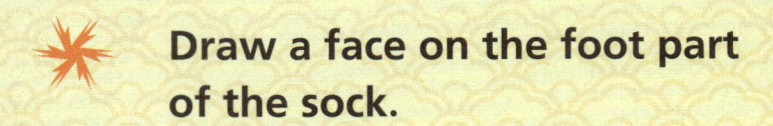

* Ask a grown-up to give you an old sock.

* Draw a face on the foot part of the sock.

* Now, stick your hand in the sock.

* Use your fingers to make a mouth.

* Move the mouth up and down.

* Make your sock say something!

READ & RESPOND

Author's Purpose

Why did the author write this text? Write two things that help you know.

_____

_____

Reread and Respond

1 **How do people make Bunraku puppets move in lifelike ways?**

_____

_____

_____

> **Hint**
> For clues, see page 68.

2 **How do you think stage scenery helps to bring a puppet show to life?**

_____

_____

_____

> **Hint**
> For clues, see page 70.

3 **What is the difference between a Bunraku puppet and a shadow puppet?**

_____

_____

_____

> **Hint**
> For clues, see pages 67 and 68.

MODULE 4 WEEK 1

To the South Seas

by Margaret Maugenest

In the late 1700s, there were few maps of the South Seas. Scientists in England wanted to know about the land in the South Pacific. Was there a huge continent there? Some people thought there was. They asked Captain James Cook to go find out.

READ & RESPOND

Ideas and Support

What clues on this page tell you that this story contains facts?

_____
_____
_____

An ocean trip was long. It was hard. There were many dangers. The seas could get stormy. Pirates could attack. A fire could break out. There was no way to get help.

Cook and his crew got ready for the voyage. They filled the ship with supplies. They took fresh water. They took food. They had a goat for milk.

Cook's Voyage

England
Tahiti

READ & RESPOND

Ideas and Support

How does the author support her idea that a trip across the ocean was long and hard?

Setting Sail

Ninety-five crew members were aboard. Each person on the ship had a certain job.

The ship left England in 1789. It sailed west. It crossed the Atlantic. It went around the tip of South America. A huge storm came up! Five of the men died.

READ & RESPOND

Ideas and Support

Does the author use any numbers on this page? What do you learn from the numbers?

_____
_____

The ship sailed for ten more weeks. The men started to run out of food. They did not want to starve. They caught fish to stay alive.

They went through the South Pacific. The men finally spotted Tahiti. The men were happy. They could not wait to reach the island. They had been at sea for eight months.

READ & RESPOND

Ideas and Support

The author says the men were happy. How does she support this idea? Explain.

_____
_____

Land, Ho!

The ship sailed into a bay. The crew dropped the anchor. This held the ship in place. Then the crew got into a smaller boat. They rowed to land.

At first, the people who lived there were uneasy. They did not know Captain Cook. They wanted to know what Cook wanted. Soon they became friendly.

READ & RESPOND

Ideas and Support

What evidence does the author give to support the idea that the people on land were uneasy?

_____
_____

Cook stayed in Tahiti for three months. He made a map of the island. His scientists studied the plants there.

Then Cook sailed on. He explored the South Seas more. He looked for a huge continent. He did not find one. Cook did see a smaller continent. It was Australia. Mapmakers now had to make new maps.

READ & RESPOND

Ideas and Support

List three facts you read on this page.

_____
_____
_____

Cook's Maps

Cook made two more sea trips. He changed old maps. He showed places where he had been. He made many new maps. He made a map of the west coast of North America. It went all the way up to Alaska.

Other explorers used his maps. There used to be many different maps of the same land. Cook's maps made travel less confusing. They also made travel safer.

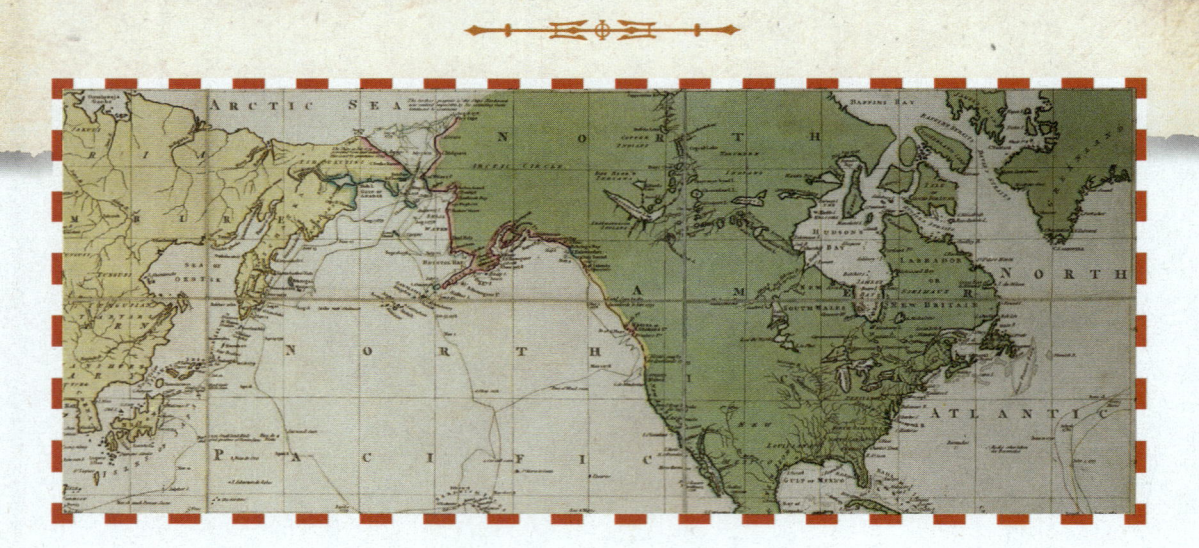

READ & RESPOND

Ideas and Support

What do you think is the author's opinion of Captain Cook? Explain how you know.

_____

_____

Reread and Respond

1 **Why did Cook set sail in 1789?**

_____

_____

_____

> **Hint**
> For clues, see pages 74 and 76.

2 **How did the people of Tahiti act towards Captain Cook and his crew?**

_____

_____

_____

> **Hint**
> For clues, see page 78.

3 **What did Captain Cook find out about the continent in the South Seas?**

_____

_____

_____

> **Hint**
> For a clue, see page 79.

Mark's Idea

by Dina McClellan

Jamal's class is learning about recycling. The kids have to do special work. They have to show how they recycle.

Jamal wants to make a video. He asks Jen, Paul, and Mark to help.

Jamal writes some notes. He talks them over with his teacher. She likes his ideas. The project is a go!

READ & RESPOND

Theme

What happens at the beginning of this story?

_____
_____
_____

Jamal and his friends go to the teachers' room. Mr. Ruiz sees them.

"What's up?" asks Mr. Ruiz.

"We're making a video about recycling," says Paul. "Can we film the trash in the teachers' room?"

Mr. Ruiz smiles. "A video about recycling? That's a great idea!" he says. "Mrs. Hill is here, too. Maybe we can help."

READ & RESPOND

Retell

Where do Jamal and his friends go first?

_____
_____
_____

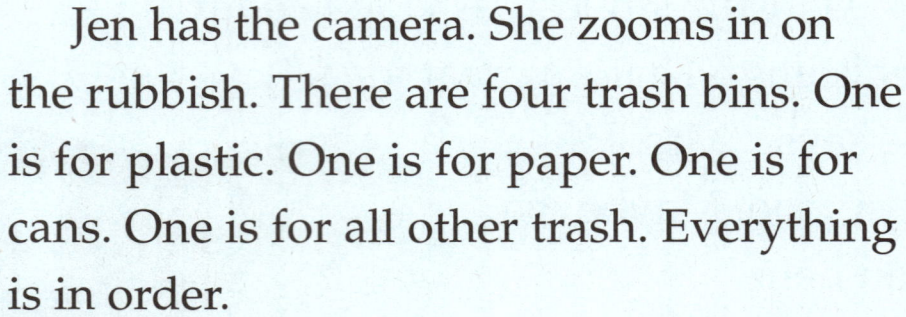

Jen has the camera. She zooms in on the rubbish. There are four trash bins. One is for plastic. One is for paper. One is for cans. One is for all other trash. Everything is in order.

Jen aims the camera at Mr. Ruiz and Mrs. Hill. They tell about how teachers recycle. When they are done, the kids thank the teachers. Then the kids leave.

"Our video has good facts. Still, I don't think it is much fun," Jamal says.

READ & RESPOND

Retell

What does Jamal think about their video?

_____
_____
_____

"Let's see how students recycle," Jen says. "That might be fun."

The kids go to the student lunchroom. Jamal has the camera. Jen and Paul smile. "Here is a bin for cans," says Paul. "Inside we see—"

Paul stops. He frowns. "I see plastic bags, bottles, and a milk carton!" he says. "They don't belong in there!"

"Stop the camera!" says Jen.

| READ & RESPOND | Theme |

What problem do the friends have?
_____
_____
_____

"The project is in trouble!" Jen says. "Kids are putting things in the wrong bins. We can't make a video about that!"

"I know what to do!" Mark says. "We don't have to just talk about recycling. We can make a how-to video. We can show how it's done!"

READ & RESPOND

Retell

Why does Jen think the project is in trouble?

_____
_____
_____

Jen and Paul stand by the bins. Mark turns on the camera.

"Bags and cartons don't go with cans," Paul says. "We can show how to recycle the right way!"

Jen and Paul pick up some trash. They put it in the right bins.

Jamal smiles. "This is more fun," he says. "Our video will be great!"

READ & RESPOND

Retell

Retell the story in your own words.

_____
_____
_____

87

What Is Made from Recycled Materials?

- ♻ From **paper** we get newspapers, cereal boxes, and wrapping paper.

- ♻ From **plastic** we get tables, benches, bike racks, cameras, backpacks, shoes, and clothes.

- ♻ From **glass** we get jars and tiles.

- ♻ From **rubber** we get bulletin boards and playground equipment.

- ♻ From **steel** we get cans, bicycles, cars, and nails.

READ & RESPOND

Theme

Why do you think the author wrote this list?

_____
_____
_____

Reread and Respond

1 **What did you learn about recycling from this story?**

_____

_____

_____

> **Hint**
> For clues, see pages 84, 85, and 88.

2 **Why do the students end up making a how-to video?**

_____

_____

_____

> **Hint**
> For clues, see pages 85 and 86.

3 **Does the author think recycling is important? Explain why or why not.**

_____

_____

_____

> **Hint**
> Your answer to questions 1 and 2 should help you.

THE Rockets

by Candyce Norvell

It was the beginning of the season. Coach Gema was giving the Rockets a speech.

"There are three things we need for a winning team," he said. "We need practice. We need discipline. We need teamwork. I want you all to work with the team. Don't try to be a star on your own. Remember, there's no *I* in *team*."

READ & RESPOND

Theme

Why does Coach Gema want the Rockets to remember that there is no *I* in *team*?

_____

_____

The team worked hard at practice. Soon they were working well as a team. They even won their first game!

Coach Gema was proud. Then he heard some team members brag. "I don't like bragging. Remember what I told you," he said. "There is no *I* in *team*."

READ & RESPOND

Theme

Why doesn't Coach Gema want the team members to brag?

_____
_____
_____

One day, Emily told her friend Lupe bad news. Emily had to quit the team. "My mom is sick," Emily said. "My family needs me at home. We all need to help out. We can't afford to pay someone else."

"The team will be sorry to lose you," said Lupe. "You are a great player."

Lupe told the team about Emily.

"I am worried about Emily and her family," said Will. "Can the team help?"

READ & RESPOND Main Ideas and Details

What is the problem in the story?

_____

_____

_____

"I know a group that helps families," Anders said. "Maybe we can raise money for that group."

"That's a great idea," said Coach Gema. "What should we do?"

"How about a car wash?" said Sovann. "We could have it this weekend."

The whole team agreed.

Charity Car Wash
This Saturday
Wash & Dry
$3.00

READ & RESPOND

Main Ideas and Details

How is the team trying to solve the problem?

_____
_____
_____

On Saturday, the team brought supplies. They washed cars all day. They raised a lot of money. They gave the money to the group that would help Emily's family.

Coach Gema was proud of the Rockets. "You remembered that there is no *I* in *team*," he said.

"Maybe we can earn more money. Let's have a car wash next weekend, too," said Anders.

READ & RESPOND

Theme

This is the third time the author uses the phrase "there is no *I* in *team*." Why do you think that is?

_____
_____

When the season ended, the Rockets went to the school sports dinner.

"There are two more awards to give out," said the principal. "One award is for a team that raised money to help someone. The other award is for the best teamwork. Both awards go to the Rockets! They remembered that there's no *I* in *team*."

Everyone clapped. The Rockets listened to the applause. They were proud.

> **READ & RESPOND** Theme
>
> **What did the Rockets remember? Why is that important?**
>
> _____
>
> _____
>
> _____

Later that week, the Rockets went out for pizza.

"I want olives!" said Anders.

"I want extra cheese!" said Lupe.

"I want hot peppers!" Sovann said.

"Not peppers! I want sausage," said Will.

"Hey!" said Coach Gema. "What about teamwork?"

"Coach," Will said, "there is no I in *team*, but there is certainly an I in *pizza*!"

READ & RESPOND

Theme

How does the story end? What do you think is the theme of the story?

_____
_____
_____

Reread and Respond

1 How do you know that Lupe is a good friend to Emily?

_____

_____

_____

> **Hint**
> For clues, see page 92.

2 What shows you that the Rockets know how to work as a team?

_____

_____

_____

> **Hint**
> For clues, see pages 91 and 94.

3 Would you like to play for the Rockets? Why or why not?

_____

_____

_____

> **Hint**
> Think about how the team members treat each other.

MODULE 5 WEEK 1

Little Mud-Face
An American Indian Cinderella Tale

retold by Dina McClellan

Long ago, a hunter and his three daughters lived near a lake. Oldest Sister and Middle Sister were mean to their little sister. They made her do all the work.

The little sister had to cook and clean. She carried heavy sticks for the fire. Her face and arms were always dirty. People called her Little Mud-Face.

READ & RESPOND

Literary Elements

When and where does this story take place?

_____
_____
_____

Across the lake was the wigwam of Strong Wind and his sister, Bright Eyes. Bright Eyes loved her brother very much. She could see and hear him. Most other people could not.

One day, Bright Eyes came to the village. "Strong Wind and I are looking for someone to join our happy family," she said. "Only someone who tells the truth may live with us."

READ & RESPOND

Literary Elements

Why does Bright Eyes come to the village?

_____
_____
_____

Oldest Sister put on her best clothes. She found Bright Eyes by the lake.

"Strong Wind is out fishing," said Bright Eyes. "Can you see him in his canoe?"

"Of course I can," said Oldest Sister.

"What is his bowstring made of?" Bright Eyes asked.

"The hide of a deer," said Oldest Sister.

"Go home now," said Bright Eyes.

READ & RESPOND

Literary Elements

Why does Bright Eyes tell Oldest Sister to go home?

_____
_____
_____

The next day Middle Sister set off. She, too, found Bright Eyes by the lake.

"Do you see my brother near his canoe?"

"Of course," said Middle Sister.

"Then what is his bowstring made of?"

"Braided grass," said Middle Sister.

"Go home now," said Bright Eyes.

READ & RESPOND

Literary Elements

Describe what is happening in the story.

_____
_____
_____

101

The next day Little Mud-Face told her sisters that she would find Bright Eyes and Strong Wind. She would show them that she spoke the truth. Her sisters burst out laughing. Little Mud-Face didn't care.

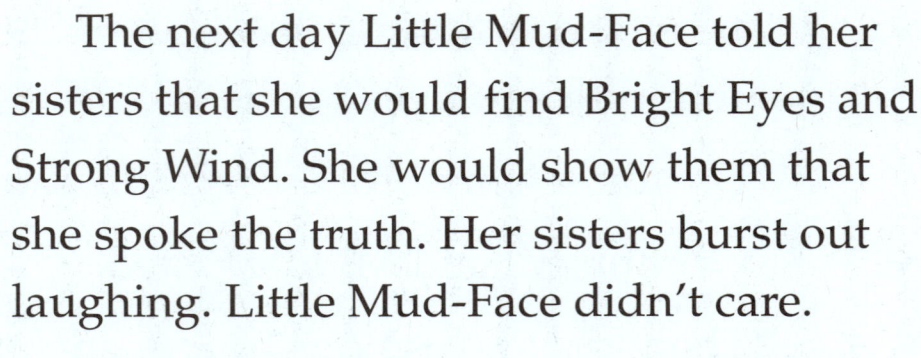

She started walking around the lake. The land was rugged. Little Mud-Face climbed steep hills. She walked without pausing to catch her breath.

READ & RESPOND

Literary Elements

What is the mood at this point in the story?

_____
_____
_____

At last Little Mud-Face reached the lake. The water was covered with mist. Bright Eyes was waiting for her.

"Can you see my brother?" she asked.

"Oh, yes," said Little Mud-Face. "How special he is! He has a bowstring made from a rainbow!"

READ & RESPOND

Literary Elements

What do you finally learn about Strong Wind?

_____

_____

_____

"You are right, Little Mud-Face," said Bright Eyes. "Only now you will be Rainbow Star." She led the girl to her wigwam. She cleaned her face and gave her a beautiful robe to wear.

Then Strong Wind came in. He looked at Rainbow Star fondly. "Someone who tells the truth will always be able to see the truth," he said. "From now on, you will be part of our family."

READ & RESPOND

Literary Elements

How is the problem resolved?

_____
_____
_____

Reread and Respond

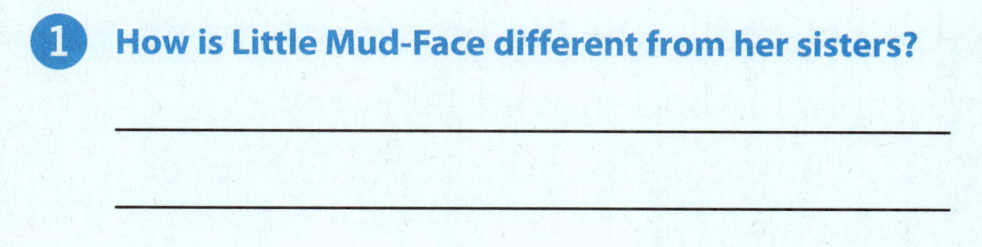

1 **How is Little Mud-Face different from her sisters?**

_____

_____

_____

> **Hint**
> Look on pages 100, 101, 103, and 104.

2 **How do you know that Little Mud-Face wants very much to show Bright Eyes and Strong Wind that she tells the truth?**

_____

_____

_____

> **Hint**
> Look on page 102.

3 **What is the theme of the story?**

_____

_____

_____

> **Hint**
> Reread the story to help you.

Dog of the Future

by Estelle Kleinman

April stared at the big box. It was from Uncle Bob. He had moved far away in 3045. That was five years ago. He never forgot her birthday.

She opened the box. Her eyes opened wide. Uncle Bob had made a robot dog for her!

A note was in the box. April read it. She grabbed the robot dog. "I'll call you Joe," she said. She loaded Joe into her speedboat. She headed for Paco's place.

READ & RESPOND

Monitor and Clarify

What year does this story take place? What clues in the text helped you to figure it out?

_____
_____

Paco didn't think much of Joe. "A bunch of tin and screws isn't the same as a real dog," he said.

"Oink!" complained Joe.

"I guess Uncle Bob still needs to work some things out. Can you come on my boat?" asked April. "Then I can show you why Joe is so great."

"Currently, I have no other plans," Paco said. He hopped on the boat.

READ & RESPOND

Literary Elements

Who are the characters in the story? Describe one of them.

_____
_____
_____

"Let's take a trip," said April. "I'll show you why Joe is a good dog."

Joe took the wheel. He steered the boat away from the dock.

"Can he really control the boat?" Paco asked.

"Yes," answered April. "Uncle Bob says I just have to punch in where we want to go." Joe had a keyboard on his back. April typed in "Tower Cliffs."

READ & RESPOND

Monitor and Clarify

Do you understand how Joe is able to control the boat? What clues in the text can help you to understand?

_____

_____

The water began to get very rough.

"Joe, I'm getting scared!" Paco cried with terror in his voice.

Joe slowed the boat to a crawl. A few minutes later, the boat stopped.

"That's not Tower Cliffs," Paco noted. "It's Rocky Bluff."

"Oink! Joe made a mistake," said Joe.

READ & RESPOND

Literary Elements

What problem do Paco and April have? How does Joe react to the problem?

"I'll tell Uncle Bob about the problems. I'm sure he can fix Joe," said April.

Joe tried again. This time he managed to get to Tower Cliffs. They all stepped onto the beach.

"Just watch the fancy tricks Joe can do," April said. "He can throw the ball and catch it!"

Paco wasn't impressed. "I prefer real dogs. They're full of surprises."

READ & RESPOND

Literary Elements

Did the problem get resolved? Explain.

_____
_____
_____

Joe picked up the ball. "Should Joe throw right or left? Fast or slow?"

"How disappointing!" said Paco. "This takes the fun out of playing ball."

"Just throw the ball!" April called.

Joe threw the ball. Then he ran to make the perfect catch.

April stopped and looked around. "What's that noise?"

Paco said, "I hear yelling and barking!"

READ & RESPOND

Monitor and Clarify

How does Paco feel about Joe? What clues in the text help you to know?

_____
_____
_____

A brown dog ran up to April and Paco. His owner, Tina, was not far behind.

April told Tina, "We were just playing ball with my robot dog."

Tina asked if her dog Max could play. Paco threw the ball. Max ran after it. He dropped the ball at Paco's feet. Before Paco could get the ball, Joe picked it up. He threw it.

Tina laughed. "Real or robot, these two dogs are a pleasure to watch."

READ & RESPOND

Literary Elements

How does the story end?

_____
_____
_____

Reread and Respond

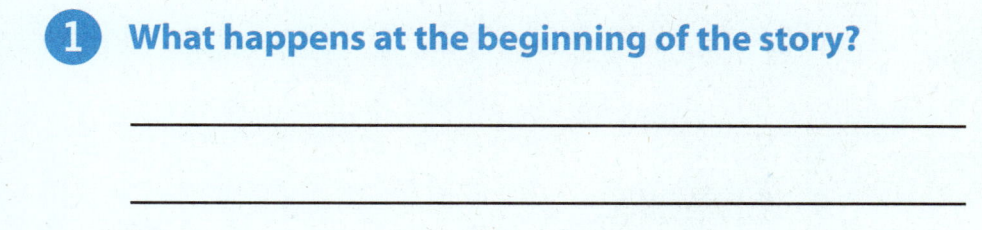

1 **What happens at the beginning of the story?**

_____

_____

_____

> **Hint**
> For a clue, see page 106.

2 **After Paco hops in the boat, what does Joe do?**

_____

_____

_____

> **Hint**
> For clues, see pages 107 and 108.

3 **Do you think Paco changed his mind about Joe? Explain.**

_____

_____

_____

> **Hint**
> Use clues in the story to make a guess.

The Race of 1903

by Dina McClellan

The first cars were made over 100 years ago. They weren't called cars. They were called autos.

Most people had never seen an auto. Automakers wanted to show off their new machines. They announced that they would hold a race.

READ & RESPOND　　　　　　　　　　Text Structure

Why did automakers have a race?

_____
_____
_____

A Race Across the Country

The Great Race took place in 1903. The race was across the whole country. It started in San Francisco. It ended in New York.

The cars in the race only had front seats. They had no windshields. The cars did not have the ability to go fast. They only went about thirty miles per hour. Still, most people thought the cars were amazing.

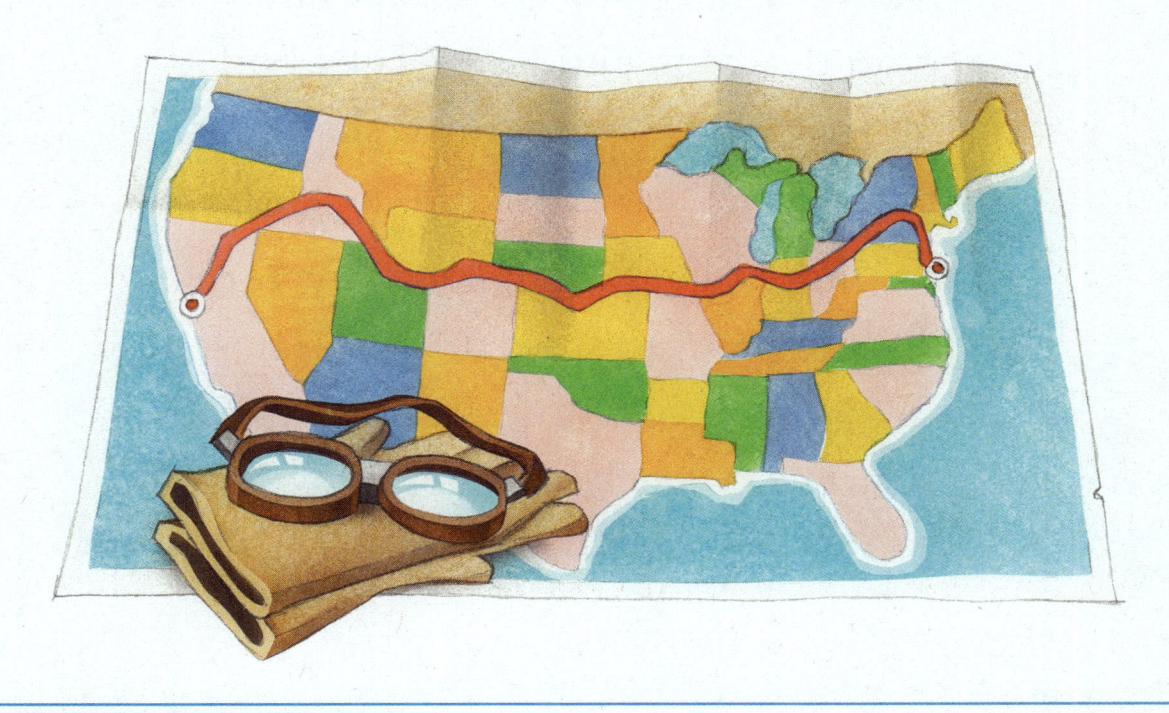

READ & RESPOND

Make and Confirm Predictions

How long do you think the race will last? What clues on this page can help you guess? Keep reading to find out if your guess is correct.

_____
_____

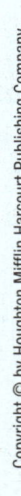

Drivers prepared for the race. They packed food, water, and tools. They had tarps for the rain. They planned the best route.

They did not want to make sharp turns. They did not want to cross ditches. Those things slowed drivers down. They wanted to go fast. There was a prize for the winner.

READ & RESPOND

Text Structure

What did drivers do to prepare for the long trip? Use the words "first," "next," and "last" in your answer.

_____

_____

They're Off!

The race began on one of the loveliest mornings in June. Crowds lined the streets of San Francisco. Bands played. The mayor gave a speech. The cars lined up. They were ready to go.

Then the cars took off! Some went off the roads. This was dangerous. A car could run into a ditch. It might break down.

READ & RESPOND

Main Ideas and Details

What took place before the start of the race?

_____
_____
_____

Rough Roads

Sometimes roads were bad. Then the drivers had to slow down. They sped up when the roads were good. The cars made the air dusty. The cars did not have windshields. Each person in the car had to wear goggles.

Cars often got flat tires. Their engines broke. Then the cars needed to be fixed. Drivers fell behind in the race.

READ & RESPOND Main Ideas and Details

What made the trip difficult? Name some things that could go wrong.

_____
_____
_____

Along the Way

People came to watch and shout advice. They cheered as the cars drove by.

Some drivers tried to collect money. They did this by giving people rides in their cars. Then they bought more supplies for the trip.

READ & RESPOND

Make and Confirm Predictions

Do you think anyone will finish the race? Why do you think so? Keep reading to confirm your prediction.

_____

_____

Reaching the Finish

The race lasted for two months. At last the drivers reached New York. They were covered in mud. They were tired. Still, they were proud.

The Great Race of 1903 was big news. It made people think that the auto was more than a neat machine. It was a great way to travel.

READ & RESPOND Text Structure

How did the Great Race of 1903 change people's thinking?

_____
_____
_____

Reread and Respond

1 **How were cars of the past different from the cars of today?**

_____

_____

_____

> **Hint**
> For clues, see pages 115 and 118.

2 **What could make drivers lose time in the race?**

_____

_____

_____

> **Hint**
> For clues, see pages 116, 117, and 118.

3 **Why was the race important?**

_____

_____

_____

> **Hint**
> For clues, see pages 114 and 120.

MODULE 6 WEEK 1

A World of Ice

by Lois Grippo

Winter at Sea

It was the winter of 1933. Louise Arner Boyd had been at sea for six weeks. Louise was an explorer. She and her team were making a map. It was of the shore of northeast Greenland. The work was dangerous.

The land was an icy wilderness. There was no sign of life.

READ & RESPOND Author's Craft

Are there any descriptive words on this page? What do those words make you see, hear, smell, taste, or feel?

_____

_____

The ship moved toward a glacier. Louise stared at the mountain of ice. She took photos. She made notes of everything she saw.

It was very cold. There was no shelter from the wind. Louise did not mind. "There is never any hardship in doing what interests you," she said.

READ & RESPOND

Author's Craft

How do you think the author feels about Louise? Why do you think so?

_____

_____

_____

Stuck!

All at once, the ship shook. Louise fell to her knees. There was a loud groan. The ship had run aground.

The captain said, "Reverse the engines!" The crew ran the engines at full speed. The ship didn't move.

They were stuck.

READ & RESPOND

Author's Craft

Remember that the mood of a text is how you feel while reading. What is the mood at this point in the text?

Northeast Greenland was a bad place to be stuck. The climate was harsh. In winter, it was the worst. Many cold and hungry explorers had died in this region.

There were no other ships nearby. There were no towns or villages. There was no one to save them. Louise and her team would have to save themselves.

READ & RESPOND

Author's Craft

Describe Greenland. Use the sensory words from the text to help you.

_____
_____
_____

125

A Dangerous Situation

The tide was getting lower. The water level went down. The crew watched. Their constant worry was that the ship would tip over. If it did, they could do nothing.

The ship did not tip over.

When the tide came back in, the ship didn't float off the mud. It was too heavy. It was still stuck.

READ & RESPOND

Author's Craft

Has the mood changed? Describe how you felt while reading this page.

Louise Has a Plan

The crew had to make the ship lighter. The men took three boats off the ship. They unloaded oil and gas. They threw coal overboard.

The tide came in. The ship was still stuck. Louise saw a big iceberg. She had an idea. The crew tied a cable around the iceberg. They would try to pull themselves out of the mud!

READ & RESPOND

Main Ideas and Details

What did the crew do to make the ship lighter?

_____
_____
_____

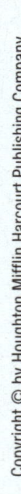

The captain ordered the crew to start the engines. The cable was attached to a crank. The engines roared. The crank pulled the cable.

The cable stretched tightly. It began to pull the ship toward the iceberg. The ship lifted off the mud! It was floating again.

Louise's plan had worked. The ship moved safely out to sea.

READ & RESPOND

Author's Craft

Remember that the tone is how an author feels about a subject. What is the tone of this text?

_____

_____

Reread and Respond

1 **What happened first, next, and last?**

_____
_____
_____

> **Hint**
> You'll need to thumb through the whole story.

2 **Why did the crew worry about the tide going down after the ship got stuck?**

_____
_____
_____

> **Hint**
> For a clue, see page 126.

3 **Would you like to explore a region like northeast Greenland? Explain.**

_____
_____
_____

> **Hint**
> Details about the region are on pages 122, 123 and 125.

Mammoths
Long Ago and Today

by Candyce Norvell

Our world is full of big animals. Still, no beast on land today is as big as a mammoth. Mammoths lived in the past.

Many mammoths lived during the Ice Age. Much of the land on Earth was frozen. Mammoths had to be tough to stand the cold. They had thick coats of hair. They had body fat to keep them warm. A mammoth weighed about 6,000 pounds.

READ & RESPOND

Central Idea

Write two details that show that mammoths were large, tough animals.

_____
_____
_____

Plant Eaters

Mammoths did not hunt other animals. They were plant eaters. They used their trunks to get tree leaves. They pulled plants from the ground, too. They used large, flat teeth to grind up the plants.

A mammoth's trunk had other uses, too. It gave mammoths a great sense of smell. It let them move rocks and trees out of the way. Mammoths may have locked trunks to say hello.

READ & RESPOND

Central Idea

How did mammoths use their trunks?

_____
_____
_____

Life in a Mammoth Pack

Mammoths lived together in packs. A pack had several families. Each pack had a leader. The leader was the oldest or strongest mother mammoth.

Mammoths in a pack did not always get along. They could be fierce. Sometimes they fought with their tusks. The tusks were about ten feet long. They were tough weapons. The tusks could also dig through snow to get plants.

READ & RESPOND Central Idea

What do you think is the most important idea on this page? How does the heading help you know?

_____

_____

Mammoths and People

People hunted mammoths. Hunters fought the beasts with stone weapons. They ate the meat. They used the bones to make weapons and tools.

Experts think that hunters prized mammoths. Hunters made paintings of mammoths in caves. The paintings show mammoths as they really looked. This is evidence that hunters knew the animals well.

READ & RESPOND

Central Idea

How did people long ago interact with mammoths? How did they feel about them?

_____

_____

A Mammoth Find

Mammoths died out long ago. Even so, we know how big they were. In 1974, a large number of bones were found. They were found in a hill in Hot Springs, South Dakota. Workers wanted to put houses on the hill. They brought in big trucks. When they dug, they found giant bones! They were the bones of mammoths. Experts learned a lot from the bones.

1

2

READ & RESPOND

Central Idea

What did experts use to find out how big mammoths were?

_____
_____
_____

3 ▶

4 ▶

Long ago, this land was a deep hole. The hole was full of water and sticky clay. Maybe the animals tried to get a drink and got stuck. They tried to get out, but they could not.

Over time, the spring ran dry. The animal remains were buried. Their bones were not found for thousands of years. Now Hot Springs is one of the best places to learn about mammoths.

READ & RESPOND

Central Idea

Why is Hot Springs one of the best places to learn about mammoths?

_____
_____
_____

Mammoths in Our World Today

The last mammoth died thousands of years ago. How and why did this happen?

Experts think it got too warm too fast. Plants began to die. Then mammoths didn't have food. Perhaps hunters wiped out the mammoths. We may never know.

We study fossils to learn about mammoths. Their story can help us protect animals that live today.

READ & RESPOND

Central Idea

How are mammoth fossils helpful to experts?

_____
_____
_____

Reread and Respond

1 **State the central idea of the text in your own words.**

_____

_____

_____

> **Hint**
> Think about what the text is mostly about. Use the headings and pictures to help you.

2 **What did mammoths eat? How do you think we know that?**

_____

_____

_____

> **Hint**
> For a clue, see page 131.

3 **The author gives two reasons why the mammoths might have died out. Which reason seems more likely to you? Why?**

_____

_____

_____

> **Hint**
> For clues, see page 136.

MODULE 6 WEEK 3

Dogs That Help

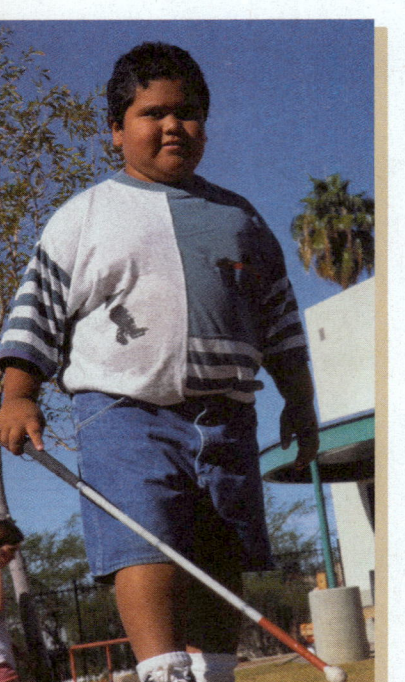

by Lois Grippo

Who doesn't love their dog? Dogs wait for us to come home. They sleep next to our beds. They bark when they hear strange footsteps. They're always around.

Being a friend is not the only thing a dog can do. For some people, a dog is an important helper. A dog can guide a person who can't see. It can nudge someone who can't hear. A dog can also bring things to a person who can't walk.

READ & RESPOND

Central Idea

Reread the last paragraph on this page. What do you think this text will be about?

_____

_____

Training

How does a puppy become a helper dog? It must go to school! These schools are special places. Dog trainers work at the schools. They teach dogs how to take care of people with special needs.

A helper dog has a lot to learn. It has to learn the difference between a red light and a green light. It has to learn how to act on a bus and with other animals. It must learn to obey its owner.

A helper dog at work

READ & RESPOND

Text Structure

Why must a dog go to school before it can become a helper dog?

_____
_____
_____

Getting Started

A helper dog must learn to do special jobs. What jobs must a dog learn? It depends on its owner's needs. Trainers make sure a dog can do the jobs that the person needs.

At last, a trained dog and its new owner meet. They learn how to live as partners. The dog helps its owner. The owner cares for the dog.

A helper dog and its owner are partners.

READ & RESPOND　　　　　　　　　　　Text Structure

What things must happen before a helper dog and an owner can meet?

_____
_____
_____

140

Seeing-Eye Dogs

Seeing-eye dogs are one kind of helper dog. Their job is to see for a person who cannot.

A seeing-eye dog helps its owner at home and outdoors. The dog leads its owner from place to place. It does not walk too fast or too slow. It protects its owner.

Seeing-eye dogs are smart. They stop when they see a red light. They lead their owner across a street when the light turns green.

READ & RESPOND

Central Idea

How do seeing-eye dogs help their owners?

_____

_____

_____

Hearing for an Owner

Sounds give information. Many give a warning. Babies cry. Horns honk. Alarms ring. Some people do not have the ability to hear. They won't know if there is trouble.

Some dogs are trained to hear for their owners. They are taught to listen for different sounds. The dog may be sleeping or lying down. When there is a noise, the dog jumps into action. It runs to its owner. It alerts him or her to the sound.

READ & RESPOND

Text Structure

How is a seeing-eye dog similar to a hearing dog? How are they different?

_____

_____

Heroes

Some people are unable to walk. They can use a wheelchair. However, there are still some things they may need help with.

Dogs can be trained to help these people. The dogs are taught to pick things up. They learn to turn lights on and off. They are even trained to push a wheelchair.

Helper dogs are heroes and loyal friends. They serve people with special needs. What do they ask for in return? Nothing more than a meal and a pat on the back!

READ & RESPOND

Central Idea

What is the central idea of the text?

_____
_____
_____

Caring for a Dog

Dogs take care of people. People need to know how to take care of dogs.

- Dogs need to run. Be sure to take your dog outside at least two times each day.

- Dogs need to visit the doctor, just like people. They need special shots to help them stay healthy.

- Keep your dog clean. Brush its coat. Give your dog a bath.

- Feed your dog healthy food. Be sure to give your dog plenty of water, too.

- Be as loving and loyal to your dog as your dog is to you!

READ & RESPOND

Text and Graphic Features

Why do you think the author wrote this information in a list?

_____
_____
_____

Reread and Respond

1 **Do you think the author wrote this story to persuade the reader to get a helper dog? Why or why not?**

_____

_____

_____

> **Hint**
> Clues you can use are on almost every page. For example, see pages 139 and 141.

2 **What are two things a helper dog might do for a person who can't walk?**

_____

_____

_____

> **Hint**
> For clues, see page 143.

3 **What are two ways that a person can take care of a dog?**

_____

_____

_____

> **Hint**
> For clues, see page 144.

Climbing the Slopes

by Mia Lewis

It is a sunny day in the Green Mountains. A group of students arrive at a lodge. The landscape is beautiful.

"Hi!" says a young man. "I'm Javier. This is Karen. We are going to teach you about rock climbing. We'll also teach you how to find your way in the forest. You'll have a lot of fun this week!"

READ & RESPOND

Point of View

Who is telling this story? How do you know?

_____
_____
_____

The group meets inside a building. It has a climbing wall. The wall looks like a rock. The wall has different textures.

"There's a lot to learn," says Karen. "We're going to practice first."

"That wall is too steep," says Teo.

"You'll do fine," says Javier. "You just have to practice."

READ & RESPOND

Main Ideas and Details

What is the group learning how to do?

_____
_____
_____

The kids go outside. They hike along a trail. They eat their lunch in a clearing. They are hungry. The food tastes great! Karen puts a stick in the ground.

"What are you doing?" asks Maya.

"I'm going to find out where north, east, south, and west are," she says.

"My cell phone is better. It can show where we are. It has maps," says Teo.

READ & RESPOND

Point of View

What pronouns do you see on this page? What do they tell you about the point of view?

_____
_____

"A cell phone could lose power," says Latoya. "Then it can't help at all."

"We can use the sun to tell directions," says Karen. "See the shadow of the stick? Let's mark the tip of the shadow with a pebble. Now we wait awhile."

READ & RESPOND

Main Ideas and Details

What is the problem with depending on Teo's cell phone to tell directions?

_____

_____

149

They check after ten minutes. The shadow has moved. Karen puts a pebble where the tip of the shadow is now. She draws a line between the two pebbles.

"The shadow moved because the sun moved," she says. "The sun moves west. Shadows move east. We know which way the shadow moved. So we know which way is east. Now we can follow any directions we have!"

READ & RESPOND

Main Ideas and Details

Why does the stick's shadow move?

_____

_____

_____

The next day the students meet again. They stand at the bottom of some rocky slopes. Javier is with them. Teo looks worried.

"Are these ropes safe?" he says.

"They are very safe," says Javier. "You did well on the climbing wall. Give it a try. I'll be here to help."

READ & RESPOND

Point of View

How does the narrator know that Teo is worried?

_____
_____
_____

A few days later, it is time to go home! Time has passed too quickly.

"I learned so much!" says Maya. "I am going to miss this camp."

"We will miss you, too," says Karen.

"I wish I had time for one last climb," says Teo. "I feel as if I could reach the peak of the mountain!"

"You'll just have to come back soon," says Javier.

READ & RESPOND

Point of View

Is the story told in first-person or third-person point of view? How do you know?

_____

_____

152

Reread and Respond

1. **How do you think the story would be different if Teo were the narrator?**

   _____

   _____

   _____

   > **Hint**
   > Reread and find what Teo said and did in the story.

2. **Do you think the students had fun at camp? Why do you think so?**

   _____

   _____

   _____

   > **Hint**
   > For clues, see page 152

3. **Pretend you are Javier. How would you retell the story?**

   _____

   _____

   _____

   > **Hint**
   > Reread the story to help you. Remember to think about Javier's point of view.

MODULE 7 WEEK 2

THE TRIAL OF John Peter Zenger

by Lois Grippo

A Stamp for Eastchester

School children in the town of Eastchester, New York, want a special postage stamp. They want a stamp of a man named John Peter Zenger. John Peter Zenger was once put on trial in Eastchester. He was put on trial because he told the truth!

READ & RESPOND

Make Inferences

Why was the trial of John Peter Zenger unusual?

_____
_____
_____

An Unfair Leader

The trial of John Peter Zenger took place in 1735. America was still part of England. The governor of New York was a man named William Cosby. People in New York did not pick Cosby. He was sent from England.

William Cosby would not let some men vote. This made people in Eastchester very angry. They wanted others to know that Cosby was unfair.

READ & RESPOND

Make Inferences

Why might people want a governor they choose themselves?

_____
_____
_____

155

John Peter Zenger Speaks Out

John Peter Zenger ran a newspaper. He wrote in his paper about William Cosby. Everyone who read the paper learned of Governor Cosby's unfair actions.

Governor Cosby had Zenger put in jail! He said that the stories in Zenger's newspaper told lies. He claimed that the lies hurt him. Zenger stayed in jail for ten months before he even had a trial.

a printing press

READ & RESPOND

Make Inferences

Was William Cosby was a good governor? Explain.

_____
_____
_____

Trial by Jury

At last the trial began. A jury would decide if John Peter Zenger was guilty. Did he tell lies that hurt the governor? If he did, the jury would have to say he was guilty.

The jury heard the governor's side of the story first. They heard about Zenger's newspaper stories. They were told that no one had the right to print bad things about the governor.

READ & RESPOND Main Ideas and Details

What was the job of the jury in John Peter Zenger's trial?

_____

_____

_____

Zenger's Story

A lawyer told John Peter Zenger's side of the story. "What you heard was true," he said. "The stories in the paper did say bad things about the governor."

The lawyer didn't stop there. "However, the stories were honest," he said. "They told the truth about what Governor Cosby did."

READ & RESPOND

Make Inferences

If the stories were honest, did John Peter Zenger tell lies?

_____
_____
_____

A Big Decision

Finally, both sides were finished. The people on the jury thought about all they had heard. Then they made their decision.

It only took the jury ten minutes to make up their minds. They said that John Peter Zenger was not guilty!

READ & RESPOND　　　　　　　　　　Main Ideas and Details

Whom did the jury agree with?

_____

_____

_____

Remembering a Leader

John Peter Zenger was a leader. The men in the jury were leaders, too. They stood up for the right to tell the truth.

That is why the children of Eastchester want a postage stamp. They want to remind us of the trial of John Peter Zenger. They want to remind us of a right that keeps our country strong.

READ & RESPOND

Make Inferences

Do the children of Eastchester think John Peter Zenger was a good man? Explain.

_____

_____

Reread and Respond

1 How was John Peter Zenger a leader? Explain.

_____

_____

_____

Hint
For clues, see pages 156 and 160.

2 Why do you think the jury took only ten minutes to decide that John Peter Zenger was not guilty?

_____

_____

_____

Hint
For clues, see page 158.

3 How do the children of Eastchester show that they care about people from their town's past?

_____

_____

_____

Hint
For clues, see page 154.

MODULE 7 WEEK 3

Sprinting Joyce

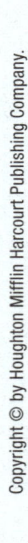

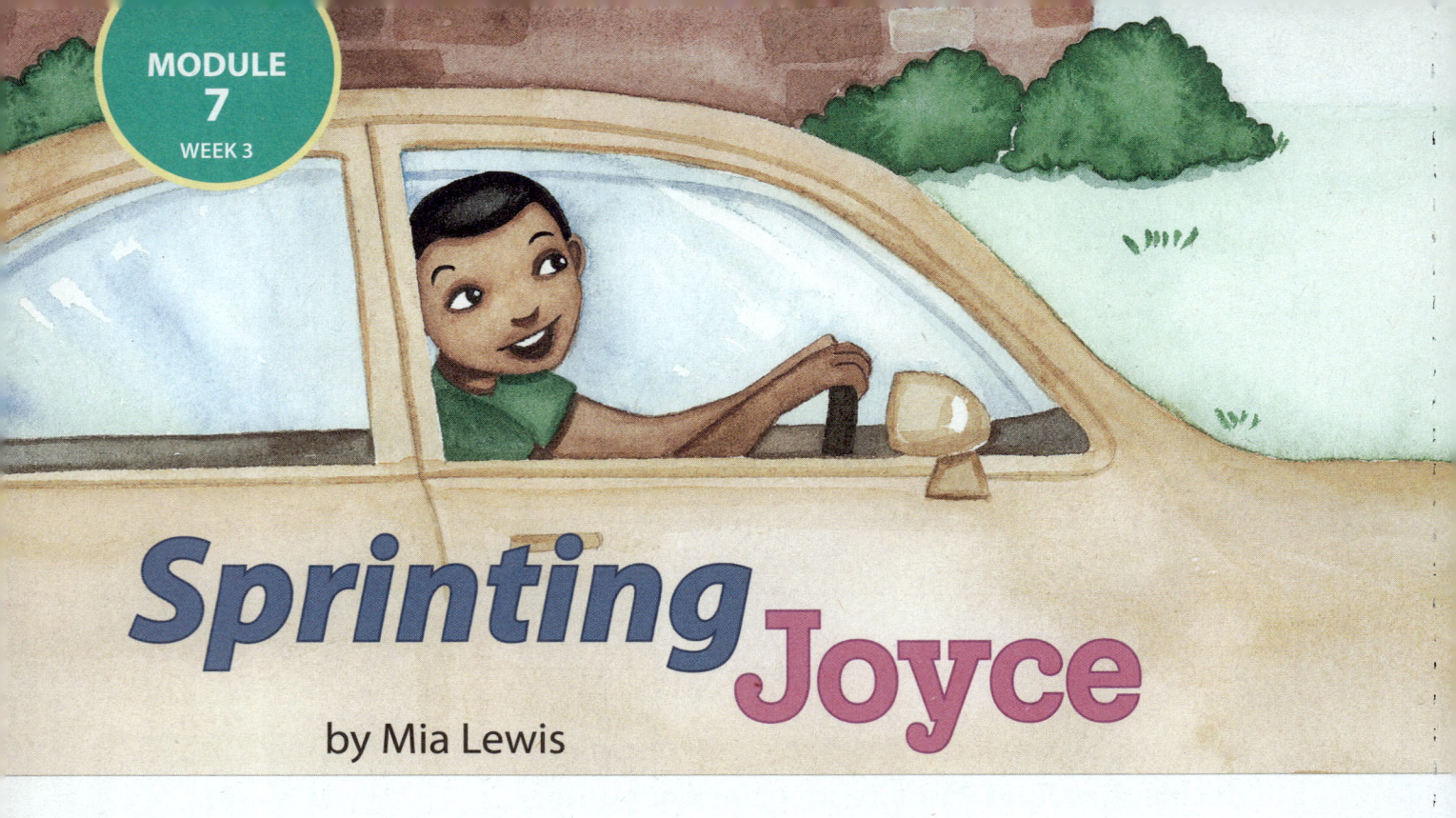

by Mia Lewis

Joyce had a big brother. His name was Roy. He drove her to school each day. When they arrived, he always said the same thing.

"See you later, slowpoke!"

This was starting to bug Joyce. She had joined the track team. Her coach didn't think she was a slowpoke!

READ & RESPOND

Figurative Language

Look at the word "slowpoke." Is this an example of a simile or an idiom? How do you know?

_____

_____

Joyce told her friend Leslie what was going on.

"Roy is the sports editor of the school paper," said Leslie. "I'll write some articles about the team. I'll give you a nickname. I'll say you are a great athlete. Roy won't know it's you. Once he finds out, he'll know you aren't a slowpoke."

Joyce smiled. "This sounds like fun!"

READ & RESPOND

Literary Elements

How does Leslie help Joyce solve her problem?

___

___

___

163

Leslie told her plan to the track team.

"From now on," she said, "Joyce will be SJ. It stands for Sprinting Joyce. Don't tell Roy!"

"Your secret is safe!" said Meg and Rita.

"You just have to run fast, Joyce!" said Leslie. "Then our plan will succeed."

"I'll try!" said Joyce.

READ & RESPOND

Figurative Language

What is the phrase "your secret is safe" an example of? What sound is repeated?

_____
_____

164

SPORTS

SJ Makes Team

by Leslie Chin

What's the buzz around school? It's about our girls' track team. They are fast, and they keep winning. They may even earn a spot at the state track meet!

The rising star is SJ. This sprinter is no slowpoke! She can contribute more speed to the team. SJ will help them win.

READ & RESPOND

Figurative Language

Write two examples of figurative language you find on this page.

_____
_____
_____

"Now I have to win!" said Joyce.

"Don't worry," said Leslie. "Just don't tell Roy how fast you run. He'll be so surprised!"

Just then, Roy walked by their table. "Who is this SJ?" he asked.

"You must be kidding!" Meg said. "Everybody knows SJ!"

READ & RESPOND

Figurative Language

Do you think Meg is serious when she says that "everybody" knows SJ? What type of figurative language could this be an example of?

_____

_____

SPORTS

Track Coach Predicts Victory

by Leslie Chin

Get set for a big win! Our girls' track team is filled with excitement. SJ is heating up the track. We're all rooting for her!

The coach is happy, too. "I think SJ will take us to the top," she said.

"I wish I could tell Roy," said Joyce. "He thinks I'm warming the bench."

"Just run," said Leslie.

READ & RESPOND

Figurative Language

What does Leslie mean when she writes that SJ is "heating up the track"? What type of figurative language is she using?

_____

_____

It was time for their next race. Joyce led the team to a big win.

"Did you know that SJ is short for Sprinting Joyce?" Leslie asked Roy.

Roy smiled. "I won't call you slowpoke anymore," he said. "I promise!"

Joyce was happy. Leslie wrote about the race. She chose a headline for the story: "Winning Team Gets Cheers from Roy!"

READ & RESPOND

Literary Elements

How does the story end?

_____
_____
_____

Reread and Respond

1 **How does Roy bother Joyce?**

_____

_____

_____

> **Hint**
> For a clue, see page 162.

2 **Write two words to describe Leslie.**

_____

_____

_____

> **Hint**
> Think about Leslie's plan and her stories.

3 **Write three words to describe Roy.**

_____

_____

_____

> **Hint**
> Think about how Roy acts at the beginning and at the end.

4 **Write a title of your own for Leslie's final story.**

_____

_____

_____

> **Hint**
> Think about what happens in the story.

MODULE 8 WEEK 1

The Boy Who Made the TV
by Cate Foley

Have you heard of Philo T. Farnsworth? If not, don't worry. Many people are not familiar with him. Philo Farnsworth made a popular invention. He made the modern television. He was just fourteen years old when he got the idea.

READ & RESPOND

Make Inferences

Does the author think Philo Farnsworth was smart? How do you know?

Farm Boy

Philo was born in Utah in 1906. He helped work on his family's farm.

Philo's parents wanted to improve their lives. They moved the family to a new farm in Idaho. In the attic, Philo found science magazines. They would change his life.

READ & RESPOND

Make Inferences

How do you know that Philo was a hard worker?

_____
_____
_____

Philo's Idea

Philo read the magazines. He learned about something called electrons. He read about a new idea. People wanted to use electrons to send pictures through the air.

One day Philo was plowing a field. He thought about electrons. He wondered if they could go back and forth like the plow. Maybe electrons could read pictures line by line! This was a new idea.

READ & RESPOND　　　　　Main Ideas and Details

How did plowing a field help Philo get a new idea about electrons?

_____
_____
_____

Television was different then. One kind showed a picture on a wall. Philo had a new idea. He wanted to make an electron tube. It would make pictures by shooting electrons at a special screen.

Philo worked hard on his idea. He tried one experiment after another. Some of his teachers helped. They tried new ways of making the tube. The more they tried, the more they learned.

READ & RESPOND

Make Inferences

Why do you think Philo had to conduct more than one experiment?

_____
_____
_____

Success!

Finally, the tube was ready. Philo tried to send an image. Can you guess what image he sent? It was a dollar sign.

The tube worked! Philo sent a television image. It was like the ones we see today. He was just twenty-one years old. His research and testing were successful. He had made a new kind of television.

READ & RESPOND

Make Inferences

How did Philo's research and testing lead to success?

_____
_____
_____

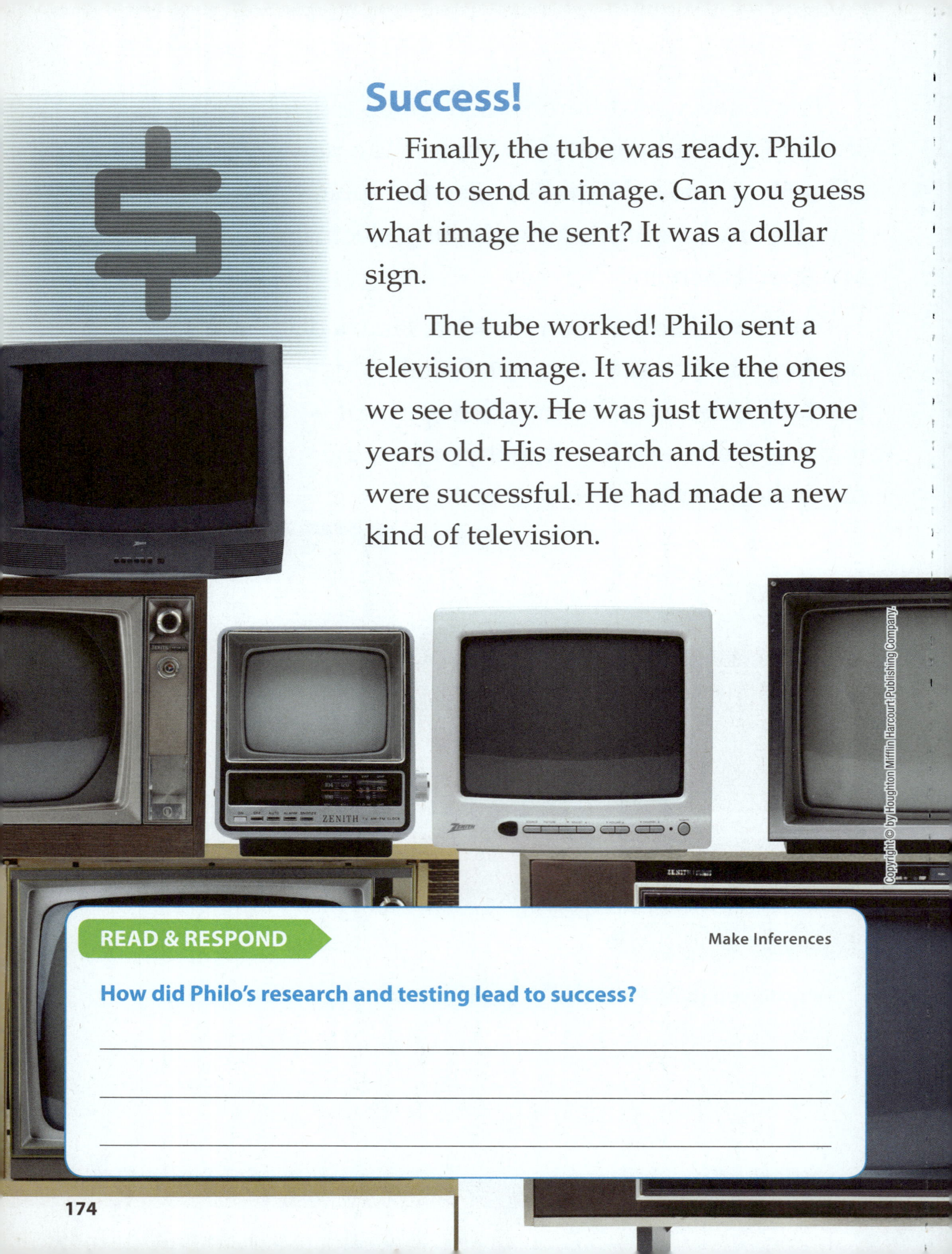

TV Catches On

Television was getting popular. A large company said that it had invented the new electron tube. A court said that Philo was the inventor.

Philo did not always like television. He thought many shows were bad. Still, television showed important events, too. In 1969, Philo saw the first man walk on the Moon. Before, he would have read this news.

READ & RESPOND

Make Inferences

How do you know that Philo changed his mind about television after watching the first man walk on the Moon?

_____
_____

A Great Inventor

Philo made other inventions. He helped create radar. He thought of a machine that hospitals used to help babies. He found new ways for people to get electricity. He created over 300 inventions!

Philo Farnsworth died in 1971. Today, almost every home has a television. A magazine said Philo was one of the most important people of the twentieth century. Would you agree?

READ & RESPOND

Make Inferences

Why did a magazine say that Philo was one of the most important people of the twentieth century?

_____

_____

Reread and Respond

1 **How did Philo become interested in science?**

_____

_____

_____

> **Hint**
> For a clue, see pages 171 and 172.

2 **Why was Philo critical of television?**

_____

_____

_____

> **Hint**
> For clues, see page 175.

3 **Do you think Philo cared about helping people? Explain.**

_____

_____

_____

> **Hint**
> For clues, see page 176.

MODULE 8 WEEK 2

Anansi's BAD HAIR Day

by Dina McClellan

Anansi the Spider was once a very handsome fellow. He had a beautiful head of thick, glossy hair.

But he was very lazy. If it was up to him, he'd lounge around in his web all day while his wife worked picking corn.

"I'm tired of doing all the work around here," Anansi's wife said to him one day. "Why don't you pick corn for a change? Besides, I'm making bean stew."

READ & RESPOND

Make and Confirm Predictions

Think about the details on this page. What lesson might this story teach? Do you think Anansi will still have hair by the end of the story?

_____

_____

Anansi sniffed. The stew smelled divine. "I can't work when I'm hungry," he sulked. Nevertheless, he grabbed his hat and started out.

The path was hot and dusty. Only the thought of his wife's delicious bean stew kept him going.

By the time he got to the field, though, all he could think about was the stew simmering in the pot. He turned and ran back home.

READ & RESPOND

Literary Elements

What makes Anansi run back home?

_____
_____
_____

"When do we eat?" Anansi hollered as he came into the kitchen.

"When you finish picking the corn." Anansi's wife scowled.

Anansi sighed. He returned to the field. He started working. But soon enough the delicious smell of the stew drifted across the field.

READ & RESPOND

Make and Confirm Predictions

Do you think Anansi will stay in the field or go back home? Explain.

_____
_____
_____

It was a smell that was impossible to ignore. He turned away and wrapped his kerchief over his face. Nothing worked. Anansi felt faint.

Just then, he spotted his wife across the field. She was carrying a bowl.

"At last!" cried Anansi, sprinting across the field toward her. He grabbed the bowl and gulped from it greedily.

"*Yecccch!*" Anansi cried, spitting it out. "But this is just water! Where's the stew?"

"Not ready yet. It will be done when you are," snapped Anansi's wife.

READ & RESPOND

Literary Elements

What is Anansi's problem? How does he attempt to deal with it?

_____
_____
_____

"Go back to work. I don't want to see you until suppertime."

As soon as the coast was clear, Anansi scurried back home. The kitchen was deserted, save for the bean stew bubbling in the pot.

"*Yum!*" Anansi cried. He grabbed a wooden spoon and started slurping hot soup. It was risky, but it was worth it.

After a few slurps, Anansi decided that spoonfuls were not enough. He pulled off his hat and filled it to the brim with steaming soup.

Just then his wife walked in.

READ & RESPOND

Make and Confirm Predictions

What do you think Anansi will do with his hat full of soup?

_____
_____
_____

Anansi froze. Then, without thinking, he tugged the bean-filled hat onto his head.

Anansi's wife looked at him suspiciously.

Underneath Anansi's hat, the soup started to burn his head. He shook his hat a little, then shook it a little faster. It didn't help. His head was really burning now. Anansi jumped. He danced. He jiggled.

"What in the world is wrong with you?" Anansi's wife said.

"Why," Anansi cried, "you don't know today is Hat-Shaking Day?"

"Nope. Never heard of it," she said.

READ & RESPOND

Literary Elements

What is happening to Anansi?

_____
_____
_____

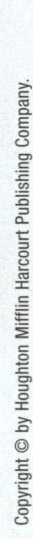

When Anansi could stand it no longer, he ripped off his hat.

"YEEEEEEeeeeow!"

Anansi went hooting and hollering down the path. He was quite a sight. The stew had completely burned off his hair. He was as bald as a kernel of corn.

Anansi's hair never grew back. That is why, to this day, he can be seen hiding out in the tall grass where no one can see his big, bald head.

READ & RESPOND

Literary Elements

What is this story meant to teach us?

_____
_____
_____

Reread and Respond

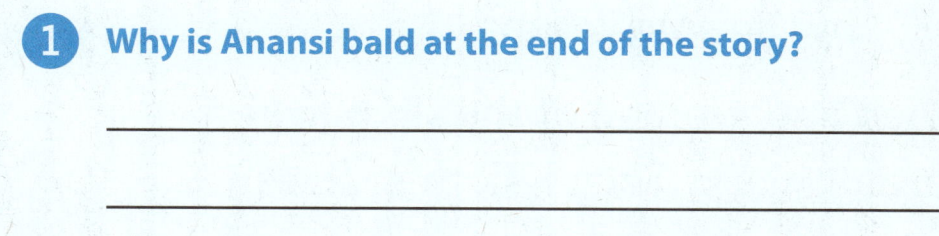

1 Why is Anansi bald at the end of the story?

_____
_____
_____

Hint
For a clue, see page 184.

2 How are Anansi and his wife different from one another?

_____
_____
_____

Hint
Think about their attitudes about work.

3 Make up your own title for the story.

_____
_____
_____

Hint
Think about the story's lesson.

4 How does the dialogue help you understand the characters?

_____
_____
_____

Hint
Think about what the dialogue reveals about the relationship between Anansi and his wife.

185

MODULE 8 WEEK 3

Ski Patrol

by Dina McClellan

The men and women of the ski patrol do important work. They risk their lives to keep people safe.

Blizzards

One job of the ski patrol is to help people in blizzards. Blizzards are bad news for skiers. Strong winds can make skiers fall. Ice and snow make it hard for them to see.

READ & RESPOND

Identify Claim

Reread the first two sentences. What is the author's claim? Remember that a claim is an opinion.

_____
_____

Avalanches

Avalanches happen when a huge chunk of snow slides down a mountain. People can get trapped inside the snow. They need help to get out.

The ski patrol has dogs. They are trained to find people in the snow. First the dogs find where the people are trapped. Then the ski patrol works fast to dig them out.

READ & RESPOND

Identify Claim

What evidence does the author give on this page to support her claim that the men and women of the ski patrol risk their lives?

_____

_____

What happens after a person is dug out? The person may be hurt. The ski patrol is trained to do first aid. They give care on the spot.

Some hurt people need even more help. The ski patrol moves these people off the slopes. They use helicopters, sleds, and snowmobiles. They get people to a hospital fast!

READ & RESPOND

Identify Claim

How does the information on this page help the author prove her claim?

_____
_____

Snow Gear

The men and women of the ski patrol have special equipment. They always wear bright clothing. That way people can recognize them.

Skiers should wear bright clothing, too. If they are lost, bright clothing increases their chances of being seen. Then they can get help.

| READ & RESPOND | Main Ideas and Details |

Why should people wear bright clothing in the snow?

_____

_____

_____

Ski Patrol Schedule

Mornings are busy for the ski patrol. They check mountain trails. They mark spots that aren't safe. They warn people about dangers that may occur at such a high altitude.

During the day, the ski patrol checks trails again. They look to see if anyone is lost, hurt, or trapped.

READ & RESPOND

Identify Claim

Does the information on this page support the author's claim that the ski patrol does important work? Explain.

_____
_____

The ski patrol works long hours. They must be sure that every skier is off the mountain at the end of the day. They make sure everyone is safe.

Only then can they rest!

READ & RESPOND

Identify Claim

Explain how this information connects to the author's claim.

_____
_____
_____

Things a Skier Might Need

Large orange plastic bag
This can attract attention. You can also climb into it to stay dry.

Ski helmet
This can protect your head while you ski.

Whistle
This can attract attention. Three blasts is a signal for help.

Compass
This helps you find your way if you are lost.

Goggles
These are important for seeing in the bright snow.

Fleece vest
This helps you stay warm.

READ & RESPOND

Text and Graphic Features

Why do you think the author wrote this information in a list?

_____
_____
_____

Reread and Respond

1. What do the headings in this text tell you about?

   _____

   _____

   _____

   Hint
   To answer this question, look on pages 186, 187, 189, and 190.

2. What is page 187 mostly about?

   _____

   _____

   _____

   Hint
   Look at the heading.

3. How does the ski patrol help people who are hurt?

   _____

   _____

   _____

   Hint
   For a clue, see page 188.

MODULE 9 WEEK 1

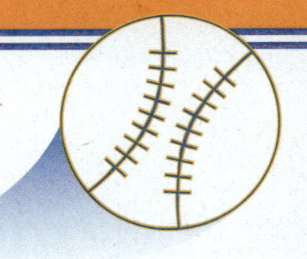

Let's Play Ball!

by Lois Grippo

Baseball for Kids

Kids all over the United States love to play baseball. Most towns have a league for children. Teams play baseball in the spring and summer.

Boys and girls play on the teams. They play other teams from nearby towns. The players' friends and families watch from the stands.

READ & RESPOND

Synthesize

Write one thing you know about baseball or one thing you want to learn about baseball.

_____

_____

The Beginning of Little League

Baseball leagues for kids did not always exist. A man named Carl Stotz started the Little League about 70 years ago. Carl loved baseball. He thought baseball was good for kids. It was a great way to teach teamwork.

Carl's neighbors thought so, too. They raised $35 to start three teams. They got stores to donate uniforms. Carl called it the Little League.

READ & RESPOND

Central Idea

Who started Little League? Why did he start it?

_____
_____
_____

Little League Then and Now

The very first Little League game was played on June 6, 1939. The Lundy Lumber team played against the Lycoming Dairy team. Lundy Lumber won.

Today, Little League teams play in every state. They play in 80 countries, too. Little League is the biggest organized sports program in the world.

READ & RESPOND

Synthesize

Write one thing you learned about Little League that you did not know before.

_____
_____

Learning Skills

Baseball players learn many skills. They must hit the ball with the bat. They must run fast around the bases. Players need to catch balls. They have to tag runners and throw the ball to other players.

One player can't win a game alone. Kids learn to work as a team. They practice, and they get better. They learn to count on each other.

READ & RESPOND

Synthesize

Did the information on this page give you a different way of thinking about baseball? Explain.

_____

_____

Going to the Big Leagues

Some great baseball players got started in Little League. One of them was Cal Ripken, Jr. He played for the Baltimore Orioles.

Baltimore fans loved Ripken. They cheered when the announcer said his name. Ripken played in 2,632 straight games! He is in the Baseball Hall of Fame.

READ & RESPOND

Central Idea

Is this information important to understanding the central idea? Why, or why not?

_____

_____

Life After Little League

Many Little League players do not become great baseball players. Some go on to do other important work. Krissy Wendell became a great hockey player. Her team won a silver medal in the Olympics.

Little League teaches teamwork skills. People can use these skills all their lives. Little League players can become teachers, firefighters, nurses, and engineers. They can do any job working with other people.

READ & RESPOND

Synthesize

Think about what you have learned about Little League. How do the skills learned in Little League help people all their lives?

_____
_____

Who Can Belong to Little League?

- Boys and girls, ages nine to twelve, can join.
- At first, just boys could play.
- After 1974, girls could join, too.

Little Leaguers in the Baseball Hall of Fame

Nolan Ryan: Pitcher, Texas Rangers

Tom Seaver: Pitcher, New York Mets

Carl Yastrzemski: Outfielder, Boston Red Sox

Johnny Bench: Catcher, Cincinnati Reds

Roberto Alomar: Infielder, Toronto Blue Jays

READ & RESPOND

Central Idea

What is the central idea of the text?

_____
_____
_____

Reread and Respond

1 **How do you think fans affect the way teams play baseball?**

_____

_____

_____

> **Hint**
> Think about how you feel when people cheer you on.

2 **Why did Carl Stotz think baseball was good for kids?**

_____

_____

_____

> **Hint**
> For a clue, look on page 194.

3 **How can you tell that Carl's neighbors thought Little League was a good idea?**

_____

_____

_____

> **Hint**
> Look on page 195.

MODULE 9
WEEK 2

Aleck's Big Ideas

by Candyce Norvell

Inventions and Inventors

Think of great inventions of the last one hundred years. The telephone, television, car, and computer are a few of them.

We know how amazing these things are. What about the people who made them? An inventor can be as amazing as his or her invention. This is the story of one amazing inventor.

READ & RESPOND

Ask and Answer Questions

Write one question you have after reading this page. Start your question with "who."

_____
_____

202

A Boy Named Aleck

In 1847, a boy named Aleck was born in Scotland. He became interested in sound.

One day Aleck got lost. He heard his father calling him from far away. This made Aleck curious about how sound traveled.

As a joke, Aleck and his brothers made a machine. It sounded like a baby crying. Their neighbors thought it was a real baby!

READ & RESPOND

Main Ideas and Details

What made Aleck think about how sound traveled?

_____
_____
_____

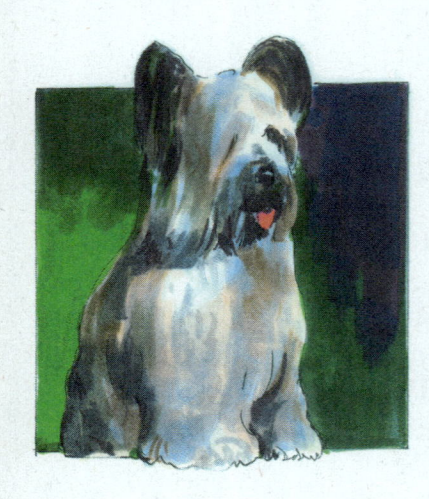

Early Experiments

Aleck tried new experiments. He even taught his dog to talk! He rubbed its voice box. He moved its jaws. The sounds that came out were like words. Soon the dog could say, "How are you, grandmamma?"

When Aleck was 14, he made a useful machine. Until then, farmers had to take the shell off wheat. Only then could people eat it. The young genius made a machine that did this job.

READ & RESPOND　　Ask and Answer Questions

Write one question you have after reading this page. Start your question with "why."

_____

_____

Growing Up

Aleck's mother was deaf. Aleck wanted to help her understand the things he said. He wanted to help people who could not hear well.

Aleck went to England to study. He met scientists there. He learned about a new idea called electricity.

READ & RESPOND

Main Ideas and Details

Write a detail that explains why Aleck wanted to help people who couldn't hear well.

_____

_____

Off to America

Later, Aleck moved to the United States. He finished his studies. He then became a teacher. Aleck married Mabel Hubbard. Like Aleck's mother, Mabel could not hear.

Aleck began to work on his biggest invention. It was the telephone. Yes, Aleck was Alexander Graham Bell!

READ & RESPOND

Ask and Answer Questions

Have any of your questions been answered? Did the answer help you understand the text better? Explain.

_____

_____

Sending a Message

Aleck had an idea. He wanted to send voice messages over a wire. He and his friend Tom Watson began to try. They worked long hours in their laboratory.

During one experiment, Aleck hurt himself. Tom was in another room. Aleck said, "Mr. Watson, come here." Tom heard Aleck's voice over the wire! The first telephone message had been sent.

READ & RESPOND

Main Ideas and Details

What did Aleck and Tom try to do in their laboratory?

_____
_____
_____

Other Inventions

Aleck made many inventions. He made an air conditioner, a metal detector, and other useful machines.

Alexander Graham Bell once said, "All really big discoveries are the results of thought." Aleck must have thought a lot. He sure made some big discoveries. Every day, other people's thoughts lead to discoveries, too.

READ & RESPOND Ask and Answer Questions

Write one question you have after reading the story. What can you do to find your answer?

_____

_____

208

Reread and Respond

1 **What is the central idea of this story?**

_____

_____

_____

> **Hint**
> Think about what every page of the story is mainly about.

2 **Write two details that tell why Aleck was curious about sound.**

_____

_____

_____

> **Hint**
> For clues, see pages 203 and 205.

3 **How would you describe Aleck?**

_____

_____

_____

> **Hint**
> For clues, see pages 203, 204, and 205.

MODULE 9 WEEK 3

Owls

by Linda Vasquez

There are about 200 kinds of owls around the world. Some of them are big. Some are small. The biggest owl in North America is the great gray owl. It can be almost three feet long. The smallest owl is probably the elf owl. It is about as heavy as a slice of bread.

Owls feed on small mammals, insects, birds, and snakes. They can catch an animal that flies, runs, or slithers. Some owls even catch fish. Most owls hunt at night.

READ & RESPOND

Text Structure

How are the great gray owl and the elf owl the same? How are they different?

_____

_____

Hunting

There are a few reasons that owls hunt at night. They can see better at night than most other animals. They can also hear better. Their color makes them hard to see in the dark.

An owl may wait on a perch until it hears or sees a small animal. When an owl flies, it is silent. A small animal cannot hear the owl as it swoops down.

READ & RESPOND

Text Structure

What does an owl do after it sees a small animal?

_____
_____
_____

Sight

Owls have very big eyes. This helps them see in the dark. Most birds have eyes on the sides of their heads, but owls have eyes in the front. They can see exactly how far away an animal is.

An owl cannot move its eyes. Instead, it moves its head. It can move its head to look backward, even while it is flying.

READ & RESPOND

Main Ideas and Details

What are some unusual things about an owl's eyes?

_____
_____
_____

Hearing

If you look at an owl's face, you will see a circle of feathers around its eyes. These feathers send sounds into the owl's ears. It can hear sounds that people cannot.

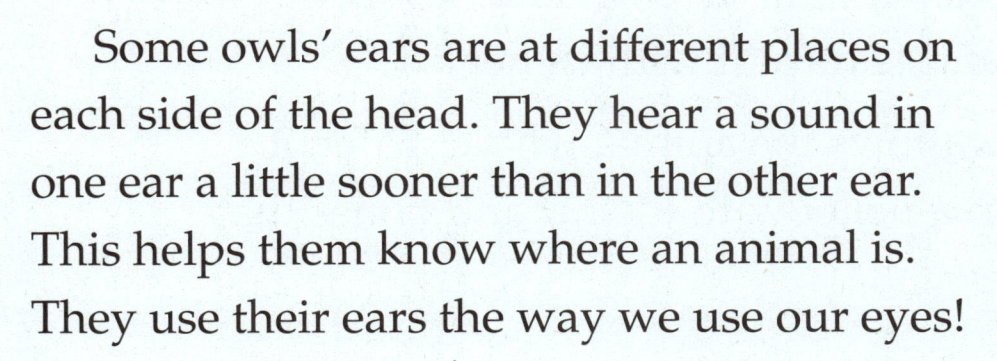

Some owls' ears are at different places on each side of the head. They hear a sound in one ear a little sooner than in the other ear. This helps them know where an animal is. They use their ears the way we use our eyes!

READ & RESPOND

Text Structure

Find two sentences that compare or contrast owls and people.

_____
_____
_____

Feeding

An owl's beak is sharp. Its claws are, too, and they are long and strong. When it catches an animal, the owl crushes it with its claws and tears at it with its beak.

It swallows the animal whole. Later, it spits up a pellet with the fur and bones that remain.

READ & RESPOND

Text Structure

What does an owl do after it catches an animal?

_____
_____
_____

Owlets

Owls do not build their nests. They may live in an old nest that another bird made. They may live in holes in trees, in ditches, or on ledges of buildings.

Baby owls are called owlets. The eggs do not hatch at the same time, so the owlets in a family may be different sizes. Owlets get very hungry. If there are owlets near you, you might hear them squeak all night as they ask for food.

READ & RESPOND

Text Structure

What causes the owlets to be different sizes?

_____
_____
_____

Who Gives a Hoot?

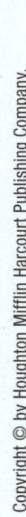

While the neighborhood dozes, owls are busy. You may have heard one hoot during the night. Or maybe you have heard an owl screech, or even whistle.

In the past, some people thought owls were very wise. Other people thought that they brought bad luck.

People today still find owls mysterious. But one thing we know for sure is that owls help get rid of pests.

READ & RESPOND Main Ideas and Details

How do people feel about owls?

_____
_____
_____

Reread and Respond

1 **Write in order the events that happen when an owl goes hunting.**

_____

_____

_____

> **Hint**
> For clues, see pages 211 and 214.

2 **Name two ways all owls are alike.**

_____

_____

_____

> **Hint**
> For clues, reread the story.

3 **What kinds of noises do owls make?**

_____

_____

_____

> **Hint**
> For clues, see pages 215 and 216.

MODULE 10 WEEK 1

SPORTS, EXACTLY

by Carl Brown

Who can sprint 100 meters in the shortest time? There is less than a second between the world's best times.

Who can throw the farthest? The difference between two excellent shot-put throws can be less than one inch.

Here's another question. How do people measure such exact amounts?

READ & RESPOND

Make Inferences

When sprinters race, does one person usually win by many seconds? Explain.

_____
_____

TIME

The first stopwatch for sports was invented in 1869. It could measure a fraction of a second. By the 1960s, new watches could measure times to one hundredth of a second.

Today, computers measure sports times to one thousandth of a second. That's how we can be sure who is the world's fastest sprinter!

READ & RESPOND

Central Idea

Why is it important in sports to measure to a fraction of a second?

_____
_____
_____

PHOTOS

It can be very hard to see who wins a close race. That's why people began to use cameras. A photo can show who crossed the finish line first.

It once took a few minutes to develop the film. People needed to improve the cameras. Now, digital photos are used. The cameras take 3,000 photos a second.

READ & RESPOND

Make Inferences

Why might it be hard to see who wins a close race?

INSTANT REPLAY

Before the 1960s, football games on television were not very popular. It was hard to see what happened on the field. That was before "instant replay."

Instant replay uses video cameras to record a game. Now, after an important play, viewers can immediately see it again. They can watch the play up close and in slow motion. People watching on television have the best seats in the house!

READ & RESPOND

Central Idea

How did instant replay change the way people watched football games?

_____

_____

BASEBALL AND TENNIS

Instant replay is also used to help the referee or umpire make good decisions. It can show if a baseball hit is a home run or a foul.

In tennis, the player has to hit the ball so that it lands inside the lines. The ball can go so fast that the athletes may not agree. Several cameras linked with a computer can show exactly where a ball hits the ground.

READ & RESPOND

Make Inferences

Why might a tennis player disagree with a referee?

_____
_____
_____

RACES

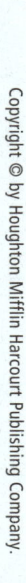

Foot races use instant replay, too. If a runner leaves the blocks less than eleven hundredths of a second after the starting gun, it's a false start. The runner must have decided to go before hearing the gun. Nobody can respond that fast!

READ & RESPOND

Make Inferences

What would happen if a runner left the blocks before the starting gun was fired?

_____

_____

SOCCER

You have read how computers and cameras help people make decisions about sports. But sometimes referees don't want to compete with machines.

Soccer games on television use instant replay. But the people who make the rules for soccer decided not to use instant replay on the field. They agree that the camera may show that a referee was right or wrong. However, they insist that a person, not a machine, should make the call.

READ & RESPOND

Central Idea

Write one way that computers and cameras help people make decisions during sporting events.

_____

_____

Reread and Respond

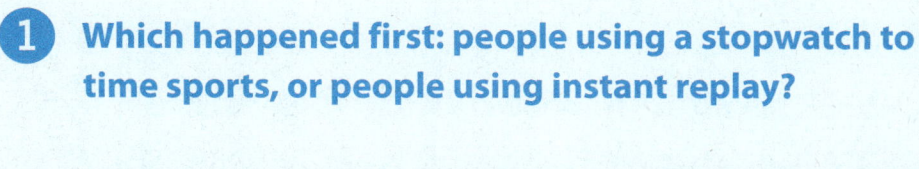

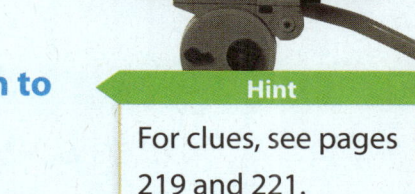

1 **Which happened first: people using a stopwatch to time sports, or people using instant replay?**

_____

_____

_____

> **Hint**
> For clues, see pages 219 and 221.

2 **Why don't soccer referees use instant replay?**

_____

_____

_____

> **Hint**
> For a clue, see page 224.

3 **Why are digital cameras more useful than film cameras in sports?**

_____

_____

_____

> **Hint**
> For a clue, see page 220.

The Jimjick King

by Dina McClellan

Once a week, Asa Dogwood and his wife, Mary, would fetch the wagon and make a long journey. They took the wagon to Bearport to pick up supplies.

Asa was always in a rush to get back, but Mary liked to stop at barn sales along the way. On this particular day, Mary saw a sign that said JUNK SALE TODAY. The sign was hanging on a barn. Mary begged Asa to stop.

READ & RESPOND

Author's Craft

What is the mood at the beginning of the story? What words help you to know the mood?

_____
_____

"Now, Mary," said Asa, sighing, "you know what's in there—the same silly things we have in *our* barn. We're always trying to get rid of the stuff!"

"Please, Asa?" Mary said. She smiled sweetly.

Of course, Asa agreed.

Together, they walked up to the farmhouse and knocked on the front door. A pleasant woman greeted them and led them to the barn.

READ & RESPOND

Author's Craft

How does the author show how Mary and Asa interact with each other?

_____
_____
_____

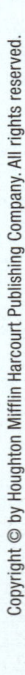

Mary picked her way through piles of old furniture, clothing, rusted farm equipment, and bad family portraits. Asa wandered off, bored.

Then Asa's eyes landed on an object he couldn't identify. He picked it up. He turned it around. He thumped it on the table. He gave it a sniff. He decided to ask the pleasant woman what it was.

"It's a—a—a jimjick!" she said.

She doesn't know, Asa thought.

He bought it for twenty-five cents.

READ & RESPOND

Author's Craft

Does the author describe the jimjick? Why do you think that is?

_____
_____
_____

When they got home, Asa showed Mary his new purchase.

"Ooooooooh! It's beautiful!" Mary exclaimed. "Um—what exactly is it?"

"It's called a jimjick," he said.

She furrowed her brow. "I've never heard of a jimjick."

"Oh, they're extremely rare," said her husband. "They can only be found here in Indiana."

READ & RESPOND

Main Ideas and Details

How does Asa try to fool Mary in this scene?

_____
_____
_____

The next time they drove into town, Mary suggested stopping at another barn sale. This time, Asa had no problem agreeing.

Another pleasant woman led them to a barn. Mary bought a painting of a prairie that looked like the view from their bedroom window. Asa bought an object very much like the first one. He batted off a cobweb and held it up.

"Another jimjick!" Mary clapped her hands in excitement.

READ & RESPOND

Author's Craft

How does the story make you feel? Is the story funny or serious?

Asa built a fancy cabinet to show off his jimjicks. Word got around. Soon Asa was known as a collector of jimjicks.

Farmers all over the county were now on the lookout for jimjicks to buy. Soon it was hard to find any. Jimjick prices went up and up to 50 dollars each!

Whenever Asa found a jimjick, he bought it. He built a much bigger cabinet to show off his new jimjicks. He now had hundreds of them.

READ & RESPOND

Main Ideas and Details

Why do jimjicks go up in price?

_____

_____

_____

Asa was recognized as the country's leading expert on jimjicks. Many newspapers printed articles about him.

Soon Asa's cabinets could no longer hold all his jimjicks. He added a special room onto his house to show off the jimjicks. After Asa died, Mary turned this room into a museum.

Unfortunately, tragedy struck. About a hundred years ago, the Jimjick Museum was hit by lightning. It went up in flames, and all the jimjicks were destroyed. Since then, jimjicks have all but disappeared.

That's why you never see any.

READ & RESPOND

Main Ideas and Details

Do you think jimjicks really existed? Why, or why not?

_____

_____

_____

Reread and Respond

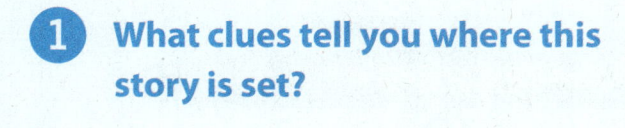

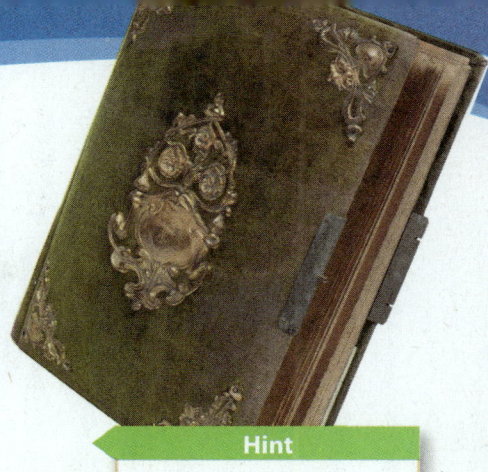

1 **What clues tell you where this story is set?**

_____

_____

_____

> **Hint**
> There are clues on almost every page!

2 **How does Asa become a jimjick expert?**

_____

_____

_____

> **Hint**
> For clues, see pages 231 and 232.

3 **What eventually happens to Asa's collection of jimjicks?**

_____

_____

_____

> **Hint**
> For a clue, see page 232.

MODULE 10 WEEK 3

The Enchanted Flute
from a Native American Legend

adapted by Dina McClellan

Once there was a widow who had a son. They lived a simple life. In the evenings they would sit and look at the mountains far away.

As the son grew older, he felt the need to roam. He wondered what life was like on the other side of the mountains.

But the boy's mother warned him: *Never go across the mountains.*

And the boy never did.

READ & RESPOND

Literary Elements

Where does this story take place? Do you think the setting will be important to the story?

_____
_____

Still, the boy was curious. He loved his mother and his home, but it was time to see the world.

His mother understood.

"A mother who ignores her son's need to see the world is not a good mother," she said. "I will not be a burden to you."

To keep her son from harm, she gave him a flute. "This is not just any flute; it is magic. Play it if you need help."

The boy promised he would. Then he left.

READ & RESPOND

Theme

Do you think the flute will be important to the story? Why do you think so?

_____
_____

After days of traveling, the boy finally reached the place over the mountains.

It was another world! A world of lush, green pastures, sparkling lakes, and fast-flowing rivers. And animals! They flew and crawled and scampered and burrowed and slithered. It was a wonder!

This is where he wanted to be. He knew he would never be happy anywhere else.

READ & RESPOND

Literary Elements

How is the place over the mountains different from the boy's childhood home? What details tell you?

_____
_____

As the boy continued walking, he found himself near a sparkling lake. He realized he was very hungry and had no food left. He would starve!

His mother's words came back to him. He took out the flute and played.

Suddenly the lake split open, and thousands of silvery fish burst out. The boy ate greedily. Afterward, he felt drowsy and lay down for a nap.

Little did the boy know that Rabbit had been hiding in the tall grass, spying on him.

READ & RESPOND

Theme

What new character has entered the scene? What do you think he is up to?

_____

_____

237

When the boy woke, he continued on his way. After a while he came to a large group by the side of a river. The Chief was speaking.

"As you know, our fish have been disappearing," the Chief said. "Without fish, we will have little to trade, and our people will scatter."

The boy spoke without hesitation.

"I am but a stranger in this land," he said, "but I think I can help." He reached for his flute.

It was gone!

READ & RESPOND

Literary Elements

What do you think happened to the flute? Why do you think that?

_____
_____
_____

"Don't listen to him!" screeched Rabbit. "He's no good! Only *I*, Rabbit, can help you!"

He held up the flute and waved it.

Then he blew into it. "*Ffffth . . . ftfff . . . Ffff!*" Nothing happened.

He tried again, more loudly this time.

"*Ffffth . . . ftfff . . .*"

In an instant, Rabbit was surrounded by a thousand angry insects.

READ & RESPOND

Literary Elements

What kind of character is Rabbit? Write a few words to describe him.

_____
_____
_____

"*Aaaaaaaa-eeeeeee!*" Rabbit yelped as the bugs bit him. In a panic, he took a leap into the river. He was never seen again.

The boy dived into the river to get his flute. He shook the water out and blew into it. All at once, thousands of fish burst out of the water and landed at the Chief's feet.

The Chief welcomed the boy into his clan. He gave him a new name, *Tcilokogalgi*, which means "the Stranger" in the Creek language.

READ & RESPOND

Theme

What happens at the end of the story? Did a character learn a lesson? What lesson did he learn?

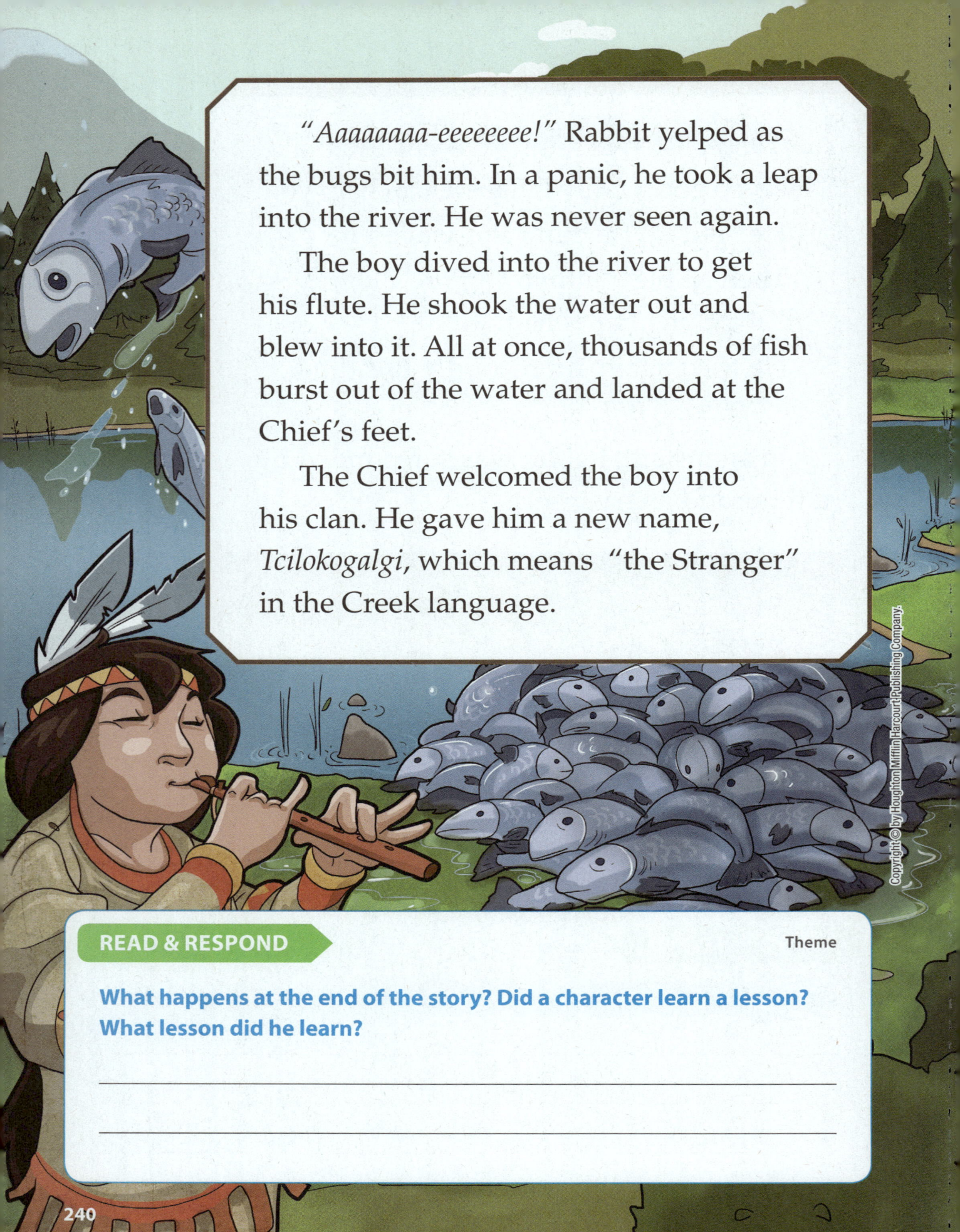

240

Reread and Respond

1 **Why does the boy's mother let him go across the mountains?**

_____

_____

_____

> **Hint**
> For a clue, see page 234.

2 **Why does the boy's flute disappear?**

_____

_____

_____

> **Hint**
> For a clue, see page 237.

3 **Why is Rabbit "never seen again"?**

_____

_____

_____

> **Hint**
> Think about the way Rabbit acts in the story.

Credits

5 *popcorn and corn* ©Stockbyte/Getty Images; 6 *milk in glass jug* ©Artville/Getty Images; 9 *basket* ©Artville/Getty Images; 18-24 *woven fabric* ©Photodisc/Getty Images; 18 *meatballs* ©Martin Rettenberger/Dreamstime; 18 *chopsticks* ©Houghton Mifflin Harcourt; 19 *measuring spoons* ©Getty Images; 19 *dumplings* ©Getty Images/Photodisc; 20 *egg shell* ©Photodisc/Getty Images; 20 *whisk* ©Stockbyte/Getty Images; 21 *leaves* ©Artville/Getty Images; 21 *cast iron skillet* ©Digital Vision/Getty Images; 22 *cannister* ©Brand X Pictures/Getty Images; 22 *garlic* ©Photodisc/Getty Images; 23 *cabbage* ©Iconotec/Alamy; 23 *measuring cups* ©Getty Images; 24 *meatballs* ©Martin Rettenberger/Dreamstime; 24 ©Artville/Getty Images; 25 *onion* ©Artville/Getty Images; 26 *right angle ruler* ©Comstock/Getty Images; 27 *crowbar with nails* ©Comstock/Getty Images; 28 *hammer* ©Photodisc/Getty Images; 29 *an expandable ruler* ©Comstock/Getty Images; 29 *hand drill* ©Comstock/Getty Images; 29 *toolbox* ©Comstock/Getty Images; 30 *vice* ©Comstock/Getty Images; 31 *plane* ©Photodisc/Getty Images; 31 ©Photodisc/Getty Images; 32 *saw* ©Getty Images; 35 *crayon line* ©Stockbyte/Getty Images; 36 *chalk* ©Comstock/Getty Images; 37 *paint set* ©Artville/Getty Images; 38 *pen* ©Phant/Shutterstock; 39 *finger paint* ©Artville/Getty Images; 42 *beads* ©Mike Phillips/Shutterstock; 43 *frog on lily pad* ©Geostock/Getty Images; 44 *frogs* ©Creatas/Getty Images; 46-47 *mosquito* ©Kletr/Shutterstock; 48 *frog* ©trutta/Shutterstock; 49 *frog on lily pad* ©Geostock/Getty Images; 50 *mountains in antarctica* ©Gerald Kooyman/Corbis; 51 *penguin* ©Gustavo Fadel/Shutterstock; 51 *seaweed in water* ©Photodisc/Getty Images; 51 *school of silver fish* ©Photodisc/Getty Images; 52 *whale with splash* ©Corbis; 53 *baby seal snow background* ©COULANGES/Shutterstock; 53 *snow petrel* ©vladsilver/Shutterstock; 53 *robin* ©Peter llewellyn/Alamy Images; 54 *flying bird* ©Alexey ©Seafarer/Shutterstock; 54 *icecaps* ©Photodisc/Getty Images; 55 *snowscape* ©Corbis; 55 *assorted black rocks* ©Photodisc/Getty Images; 57 *icecaps* ©Photodisc/Getty Images; 58 *all leaves* ©Brand X Pictures/Getty Images; 59 *squirrel on tree* ©Photodisc/Getty Images; 60 *trees snow* ©Photodisc/Getty Images; 61 *forest* ©Dmitry Polonskiy/Shutterstock; 62 *carrion beetle* ©Chris Moody/Shutterstock; 62 *forest fire* ©Corbis; 64 *frosty leaf pile* ©Photodisc/

Getty Images; 66-67 *curtain* ©Comstock/Getty Images; 69-70 *curtain* ©Comstock/Getty Images; 70 *puppet monkey* ©Hannah Gleghorn/Shutterstock; 70 *puppet show* ©Alamy; 72 *curtain* ©Comstock/Getty Images; 72 *sock puppet* ©laurien/Getty Images; 74-75 (bkgd) *sunset ocean* ©Born Traveller/Shutterstock; 74 *James Cook* ©World History Archive/Alamy; 80 *Cook voyages map* ©The Natural History Museum/Alamy; 83 *video camera* ©Lai Leng Ylap/Cutcaster; 84 *newspapers* ©Comstock/Getty Images; 85 *recycling* ©Michael Burrell/Alamy; 86 *mixed container* ©Burke/Triolo Productions/Getty Images; 87 *aluminum cans* ©1125089601/Shutterstock; 88 *backpack* ©Photodisc/Getty Images; 88 *pile of nails* ©Comstock/Getty Images; 88 *bike* ©Photodisc/Getty Images; 98 *paper* ©Oleksiy Maksymenko/Alamy; 100 *paper* ©Oleksiy Maksymenko/Alamy; 102 *paper* ©Oleksiy Maksymenko/Alamy; 104 *paper* ©Oleksiy Maksymenko/Alamy; 138 *boy with cane* ©Photodisc/Getty Images; 138 *all dogs* ©Getty Images; 139 *pointer* ©Getty Images; 139 *cocker spaniel* ©Getty Images; 139 *basset hound* ©Getty Images; 139 *newfoundland dog* ©Artville/Getty Images; 139 *affenpinschers* ©Getty Images; 139 *collie* ©Getty Images; 139 *visually impaired woman guide dog* ©Houghton Mifflin Harcourt; 140 *man with dog* ©Houghton Mifflin Harcourt; 140 *all dogs* ©Getty Images; 141 *road sign* ©Brand X Pictures/Getty Images; 141 *collie* ©Getty Images; 141 *basset hound* ©Getty Images; 141 *affenpinschers* ©Getty Images; 141 *cocker spaniel* ©Getty Images; 141 *newfoundland dog* ©Artville/Getty Images; 141 *pointer* ©Getty Images; 142 *orange traffic arrow* ©JK Jeffrey/Shutterstock; 142 *yellow traffic arrow* ©Mr. Alien/Shutterstock; 142 *all dogs* ©Getty Images; 143 *woman in wheelchair* ©Amos Morgan/Getty Images; 143 *collie* ©Getty Images; 143 *basset hound* ©Getty Images; 143 *affenpinschers* ©Getty Images; 143 *cocker spaniel* ©Getty Images; 143 *newfoundland dog* ©Artville/Getty Images; 143 *pointer* ©Getty Images; 144 *golden retriever dog* ©GK Hart/Vikki Hart/Getty Images; 145 *visually impaired woman guide dog* ©Houghton Mifflin Harcourt; 146 *back pack* ©Photodisc/Getty Images; 147 *snow boots* ©Stockdisc/Getty Images; 148 *ants* ©wizdata/Shutterstock; 149 *rock* ©Photodisc/Getty Images; 150 *compass* ©Stockbyte/Getty Images; 151 *rope* ©C SquareStudios/Photodisc/Getty Images; 152 *blue butterfly* ©Houghton Mifflin Harcourt; 152 *yellow butterfly*

©Stockbyte/Getty Images; 154 *gavel* ©Photodisc/Getty Images; 155 *William Cosby* ©North Wind Picture Archives; 155 *vote sign* ©Photodisc/Getty Images; 156 *printing press* ©Houghton Mifflin Harcourt; 156 *printing font stamp* ©Comstock/Getty Images; 157 *pen and quill* ©Vnikitenko/Dreamstime; 158 *John Peter Zenger* ©North Wind Picture Archives/Alamy; 159 *antique clock* ©Photodisc/Getty Images; 160 *hand and gavel* ©Photodisc/Getty Images; 161 ©Artville/Getty Images; 165 *newspaper* ©Feng Yu/Shutterstock; 167 *newspaper* ©Feng Yu/Shutterstock; 170 *old tv* ©Artville/Getty Images; 170 *tv with two knobs* ©Photodisc/Getty Images; 170 *retro TV* ©Photodisc/Getty Images; 170 *old TV* ©Photodisc/Getty Images; 170 *old fashioned TV* ©Photodisc/Getty Images; 171 *magazine newspaper* ©Houghton Mifflin Harcourt; 171 *old fashioned tv* ©Photodisc/Getty Images; 171 *old fashioned tv* ©Photodisc/Getty Images; 171 *television* ©Photodisc/Getty Images; 171 *tv set* ©Comstock/Getty Images; 171 *old fashioned tv* ©Photodisc/Getty Images; 171 *old fashioned television* ©Photodisc/Getty Images; 171 *old fashioned tv* ©CMCD/Getty Images; 172 *old fashioned TV* ©Photodisc/Getty Images; 172 *farmhouse* ©Corbis; 172 *tv* ©Photodisc/Getty Images; 173 *old TV* ©Photodisc/Getty Images; 173 *futuristic tv set* ©Comstock/Getty Images; 173 *tv* ©Photodisc/Getty Images; 173 *vintage television* ©Photodisc/Getty Images; 173 *tv* ©Photodisc/Getty Images; 174 *all tvs* ©Photodisc/Getty Images; 175 *early-model tv* ©Comstock/Getty Images; 175 *moonwalk* ©Stocktrek/Photodisc/Getty Images; 175 *tv* ©PhotoDisc/Getty Images; 176 *all tvs* ©Photodisc/Getty Images; 177 *retro tv* ©Photodisc/Getty Images; 178-179 *fabric border* ©Sam Dudgeon/Houghton Mifflin Harcourt; 178 *dried corn* ©Stockbyte/Getty Images; 179 *nuts and beans* ©Photodisc/Getty Images; 180-183 *cornfield border* ©Alamy; 180 *vegetables* ©Houghton Mifflin Harcourt; 181 *wooden bowls* ©Sam Dudgeon/Houghton Mifflin Harcourt; 182 *clay water jug* ©Fotosearch/Superstock; 184 *fabric border* ©Sam Dudgeon/Houghton Mifflin Harcourt; 184 *chick peas* ©Stockbyte/Getty Images; 186-192 (bkgd) *snow* ©Photodisc/Getty Images; 189 *red skis* ©Comstock/Getty Images; 191 *blue gloves* ©Shutterstock; 192 *whistle* ©Comstock/Getty Images; 192 *compass* ©Stockbyte/Getty Images; 195 *yankee stadium* ©Mike Liu/Shutterstock;

196 *baseball* ©Photodisc/Getty Images; 196 *red baseball hat* ©C Squared Studios/Photodisc/Getty Images; 196 *baseball bat* ©Corbis; 197 *baseball glove* ©C Squared Studios/Photodisc/Getty Images; 197 *baseball jersey* ©C Squared Studios/Photodisc/Getty Images; 198 *baseball* Comstock/Getty Images; 199 *medal* ©Houghton Mifflin Harcourt; 201 *yankee stadium* ©Mike Liu/Shutterstock; 206 *antique telephone* ©Comstock/Getty Images; 208 *compass* ©Comstock/Getty Images; 209 *antique telephone* ©Comstock/Getty Images; 210 *owl* ©Getty Images; 211 *animals in dark* ©Chad Baker/Digital Vision/Getty Images; 211 *mouse v*Digital Zoo/Corbis; 212 *owl* ©Comstock/Getty Images; 213 *great grey owl* ©Comstock/Jupiterimages/Getty Images; 214 *owl close up* ©Jupiterimages/Getty Images; 215 *great horned owl chicks* ©Design Pics Inc./Richard Wear/Alamy Images; 216 *snow owl* ©Corbis; 217 *animals in dark* ©Chad Baker/Digital Vision/Getty Images; 218 *all athletes* ©Comstock/Getty Images; 219 *yellow stop watch* ©Comstock/Getty Images; 219 *female tennis player* ©Comstock/Getty Images; 219 *javelin thrower* ©Comstock/Getty Images; 219 *male tennis player* ©Comstock/Getty Images; 219 *quarterback* ©Getty Images; 219 *equestrian with saddle* Comstock/Getty Images; 219 *shooting basketball* ©Getty Images; 220 *movie camera* ©Getty Images; 221 *football* ©Houghton Mifflin Harcourt; 221 *receiver catching ball* ©Comstock/Getty Images; 222 *tennis racquet* ©Comstock/Getty Images; 222 *bat and baseball* ©Corbis; 223 *runner* ©Photodisc/Getty Images; 224 *football referee* ©Comstock/Getty Images; 224 *boy playing soccer* ©Comstock/Getty Images; 225 *movie camera* ©Getty Images; 226-227 *wagon tracks* ©Brand X Pictures/Getty Images; 228 *sheet music* ©Comstock/Getty Images; 228 *antique picture frame* ©Comstock/Getty Images; 229 *rolling pin* ©Comstock/Getty Images; 229 *yarn and needles* ©Comstock/Getty Images; 229 *antique shoe mule* ©Comstock/Getty Images; 229 *compass* ©Photodisc/Getty Images; 230 *landscape painting* ©pluie_r/Shutterstock; 230 *picture Frame* ©C Squared Studios/Getty Images; 231 *window* ©WidStock/Alamy; 231 ©Charles Smith/Corbis; 232 *flames* ©Photodisc/Getty Images; 233 *antique book* ©jupiterimages/Getty Images.